AN ILLUSTRATED GUIDE TO
MODERN
SUB
HUNTERS

a Salamander book

Published by Arco Publishing, Inc.
NEW YORK

AN ILLUSTRATED GUIDE TO
MODERN
SUB
HUNTERS

David Miller

A Salamander Book

Published by
Arco Publishing Inc.,
215 Park Avenue South,
New York,
New York 10003,
United States of America.

Library of Congress Catalog
Card Number: 83-83419

ISBN 0-668-06067-0

Credits

Author: David Miller has contributed
numerous articles to technical
defence journals, and is author of
Salamander's *Illustrated Guide to
Modern Submarines,* and co-author of
The Balance of Military Power. (The
publishers would also like to thank
John Jordan whose *Illustrated Guide to
Modern Naval Aviation* was a valuable
source in the preparation of this book).

Editor: Philip de Ste. Croix
Designer: Roger Chesneau

Typeset:
Modern Text Typesetting Ltd.
Printed:
Henri Proost et Cie, Belgium

Line drawings (ships):
© Siegfried Breyer and Salamander
Books Ltd.
Profile drawings (aircraft):
© Pilot Press Ltd. and Salamander
Books Ltd.

Photographs: The publisher wishes to
thank all the official government
archives, and warship and aircraft
manufacturers who have supplied
pictures for this book. Other
photographs have been supplied by
courtesy of *Jane's Defence Weekly*
and Linewrights Ltd, and H. Kobayashi
via Captain J.E. Moore, editor of
Jane's Fighting Ships.

Contents

Vessels and aircraft are arranged alphabetically by nation of origin under separate headings according to weapon type.

Introduction

Today the oceans of the world are militarily important as never before, due principally, but by no means entirely, to the Fleet Ballistic Missile Submarine (SSBN); both superpowers have sufficient nuclear weapons at sea in these boats to destroy each other. Furthermore, submarine detection is still a very imprecise science, and so the SSBN is currently the ultimate deterrent since it provides a survivable, counter-value weapon system. Additional urgency is being lent to the anti-submarine battle by the probability that submarine-launched ballistic missiles (SLBM) may soon be fitted with manoeuvrable re-entry vehicles (MaRV), which, because they have on-board navigation facilities, will have an accuracy measurable in tens of metres, thus gaining a first-strike, counter-force role. In addition to this, however, the development of submarine-launched cruise missiles (SLCM) with nuclear warheads and a land-attack role is introducing a new threat which must be taken very seriously.

Nuclear-powered attack submarines (SSN) have introduced a major threat both to hostile submarines and to surface shipping, because they can travel great distances at great speed; not only are they more difficult to find, but they are also much more difficult to attack with any reasonable hope of success. The latest Soviet SSN, for example, is actually faster than any torpedo that can be sent against it, introducing a totally new element to the anti-submarine warfare (ASW) problems facing a fleet commander. The nature of the SSN threat was shown very clearly during the South Atlantic War of 1982 when the presence of five Royal Navy SSNs (coupled with the sinking of the cruiser *General Belgrano,* which

Below: The two basic types of nuclear-powered submarine: on the left a Los Angeles class hunter-killer (SSN)—USS *Phoenix*—and on the right two Ohio class SSBNs.

showed the intention to use them) kept the Argentine fleet within the 12-mile (19·3km) limit throughout the most critical period of the war. If the nuclear-powered boats have tended to capture the popular attention, the continued importance of conventional diesel-electric submarines (SSK) should not be underestimated. Not only are these the one type of submarine that most navies can afford, but they also have certain capabilities which the nuclear boats still cannot match.

To counter these threats from below the surface of the oceans the world's navies are spending increasing amounts of money on ASW, resources being allocated in five main areas. The first is surveillance, which covers everything from spies reporting that submarines have left port to complete satellites and vast networks of monitoring devices permanently positioned on the ocean beds.

Second come submarines themselves, which in many circumstances are the best ASW systems of all. Third is land-based aircraft, which are becoming more sophisticated and expensive, as is the fourth element, ship-based aircraft, both fixed- and rotary-wing. Finally, the multiplicity of sensors and the vast number of platforms combine to produce information in such enormous quantities that the whole question of data handling is becoming ever more pressing.

Another important consideration is that the maritime problems facing the two superpowers and their allies are quite dissimilar, because geography serves the two sides in different ways. The West needs ASW for two major tasks, to protect surface ships and to detect SSBNs. The Soviet Navy, however, does not need to protect essential convoys, and its surface task groups are, in

Below: A normal day's deployment of SSBNs: the majority are on station, a few in transit. These deployments represent the survivable retaliatory strike forces: the guarantee of peace.

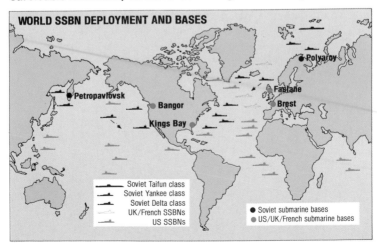

WORLD SSBN DEPLOYMENT AND BASES

- Polyarny
- Petropavlovsk
- Bangor
- Faslane
- Brest
- Kings Bay

Soviet Taifun class
Soviet Yankee class
Soviet Delta class
UK/French SSBNs
US SSBNs

● Soviet submarine bases
● US/UK/French submarine bases

THE WORLD'S NUCLEAR/CRUISE MISSILE SUBMARINES

Country	SSBNs		SSNs			SSGN/SSGs*		
	In service	On order	In service	In reserve	On order	In service	In reserve	On order
China (PRC)	1	1 + ?	3	—	?			
France	5	2	1	—	4			
USSR	73	?	73	?	?	67	—	?
UK	4	4	12	1	5			
USA	34	12	99	5	22			

*The Soviet Union is the only country to have built and deployed submarines specially equipped to fire cruise missiles. New types of cruise missile designed to be launched from standard torpedo tubes, developed in the USA and in the Soviet Union, make a specialised submarine design almost irrelevant, although the USSR is just introducing the Oscar class.

the final analysis, expendable; thus their only critical role is to protect their own SSBNs. To attack NATO SSBNs or surface task groups or convoys, Soviet ASW forces must pass through choke-points dominated by NATO, e.g. the GIUK (Greenland–Iceland–UK) gap.

Until recently ASW was a tactical pursuit, since the only threat came from torpedoes. In World War II torpedo range was at best some 11,000yd (10km), and this determined the range at which detection was necessary. Today, however, three major changes have

occurred. First, the range of torpedoes has greatly increased—the US Mk 48 torpedo, for example, has a range of some 30 miles (48km). Second, an increasing number of boats are being fitted with submarine-launched cruise missiles (SLCM): the earliest of these had an anti-ship role, but new types now entering service have nuclear warheads to attack land targets and the latest, the Soviet SS-N-21, has a range of 1,864 miles (3,000km). Third, the SLBMs now have such great range that their launch vessels, the SSBNs, do

Below: US Navy submarine-launched cruise missile (SLCM) following an underwater launch. The Soviet Navy has had SLCMs in service for some years on specially-built submarines, but the US Navy launches these missiles from torpedo tubes or special vertically mounted tubes in the submarine's upper casing.

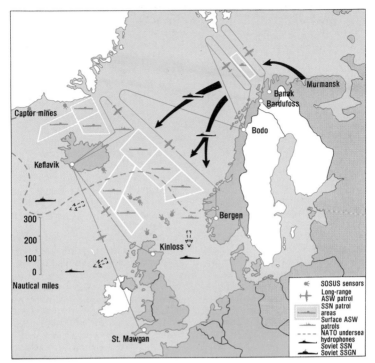

Above: This map, adapted from a Soviet source, illustrates how the USSR recognises the importance of the ASW battle to their strategic plans. Soviet SSNs and SSGNs of the Northern Fleet must transit the GIUK gap, and NATO's co-ordinated ASW platforms arrayed against them, to reach their ocean stations.

not even need to leave their own territorial waters to launch a missile against the enemy homeland. Thus whereas in World War II the ASW sphere of involvement was a circle some 20 miles (32km) in radius around a surface task group or a convoy, the area now to be covered is the entire ocean.

Many centuries of seafaring have given the impression that Man was starting to understand the oceans, but it is only now being realised that this knowledge is, both literally and metaphorically, confined to the surface and that there is actually an enormous three-dimensional world about which little is known. Indeed, more is probably known about the topography, climate, environment and resources of the Moon than about the oceans of planet Earth.

Nuclear-Powered Ballistic Missile Submarines

By far the most important underwater weapons systems are nuclear-powered ballistic missile submarines, and these are the targets of most ASW activity. It is, therefore, worth having a closer look at them and their characteristics.

Most SSBNs carry 16 SLBMs, although some of the older Soviet types carry 12, while the latest Soviet Taifun class (DoD: Typhoon) carries 20 and the US Ohio class 24. SSBNs move fast out to their patrol areas and then cruise at about 3kt, varying their depth to make maximum use of the changing properties of the oceans and thus avoid detection. Most SSBNs launch their missiles from a depth of some 300ft (91m) in a 'ripple' spread

over some 12–15 minutes, although the Soviet Taifun class has been observed firing a number of missiles simultaneously. SLBM accuracy is currently much less than that for land-based ICBMs, due to the difficulty of establishing the *precise* location of the launching submarine; SLBMs are, therefore, used against area targets (cities, industry, airfields). SSBNs are virtually untrackable in the current state of the ASW art, and thus provide both sides with a guaranteed retaliatory capability.

The main part of the US Navy's SSBN fleet is the 31 boats of the Lafayette/Franklin class, constructed 1961–66. They were all converted to take the Poseidon C-3 SLBM between 1969 and 1978, and twelve of these have been further converted to take the Trident I C-4 missile. The Ohio class are designed specifically for the Trident missile—six are now in service, with another nine building—and have the capacity to take the improved Trident II C-5 missile from 1985 onwards. They carry 24 SLBMs, and the hull design is much quieter than previous SSBNs, making acoustic detection by Soviet ASW forces much more difficult. The big increase in range of the Trident enables these boats to operate at much

greater distances from the Soviet Union and, indeed, remain in US-dominated waters.

Good management has enabled the US Navy always to keep about 55 per cent of its SSBN force at sea, and this will increase to 65–70 per cent with the Ohios. The SSBN force gives the USA the assurance of a second-strike retaliatory capability, but there is concern about the survivability of the communications system, although a high degree of redundancy gives a reasonable prospect of getting the critical messages through. Navigation and position-fixing problems are slowly being mastered; indeed, the Soviet Union is already concerned that US SLBMs may be gaining a first-strike capability.

The Soviet Yankee class SSBN appeared in 1968, a total of 34 being built. Due to the relatively short range of the SS-N-6 missile, Yankee-Is deploy close to the US coast to obtain adequate coverage of target areas such as SAC bases, a coincidental advantage being that the resulting 6–10-minute depressed-trajectory flight would prevent counter-surprise scrambles at the target airfields. Yankee-Is are being progressively converted to the attack (SSN) role to keep within the SALT-II limits as new Delta-IIIs join the Soviet fleet. Twenty-five

Yankee-Is remain, together with the sole Yankee-II fitted with SS-N-17 missiles. Eighteen Delta-I SSBNs each carry 12 SS-N-8 SLBMs; these were replaced in production by the Delta-II with 16 SS-N-8s, but only four were built as the Delta-III (14 in service) then appeared with 16 SS-N-18 missiles, the first Soviet SSBNs with multiple independent re-entry vehicle (MIRV) warheads. The first Taifun class SSBN was launched in 1980 and a further two are now building. These monsters (30,000 tons submerged) each carry 20 SS-N-20s forward of the sail in a unique arrangement, and the first is now operational. Despite having some 63 SSBNs in service, the Soviet Navy maintains only about 13 on patrol.

Only three other navies possess SSBNs. The French Navy currently has six SSBNs armed with the M-20 SLBM; a seventh SSBN is building, the M-4 missile is due to replace the M-20 from 1984 onwards, and an entirely new class of SSBNs will come into service in the late 1990s. The Royal Navy possesses four SSBNs with Polaris A-3 SLBMs, but these have been upgraded with advanced warheads under the Chevaline programme. Four new submarines will come into service in the 1990s armed with the Trident II D-5 missile.

The French and Royal Navies guarantee to have one SSBN each on patrol at any one time, but with a second frequently also at sea. The fifth navy with SSBNs is that of the People's Republic of China. The first sea launch of a Chinese SLBM took place on 10 October 1982 (CSS-NX-3), and the missile is currently being deployed in the Xia class SSSN.

In a period of tension, both superpowers would obviously attempt to deploy more of their submarines—which is why knowledge of what the other side is maintaining on station is at all times of vital importance.

Noise

A submarine moving in the ocean has a number of characteristics and produces a number of effects, some or all of which may be utilised to detect its presence. Efforts are being made all the time to refine existing methods and to discover new ones in order to make the detection and localisation of a hostile submarine quicker, more accurate and less prone to the vagaries of transitory and often capricious oceanic conditions.

The first characteristic of a submerged submarine is that it creates hydrodynamic noise, resulting from the flow of water over the hull and accentuated by protrusions and orifices such as bollards or free-flood holes. Such noise can be reduced by retractable domes, bollards, etc., and by remotely activated doors over periscopes and antennas on top of the fin. Another factor in the noise problem is that long towing wires for antennas or variable-depth sonars (VDS) may themselves vibrate at their natural frequency.

Nuclear-powered submarines have a particular difficulty with respect to machinery noise, owing to unbalanced rotating parts (turbine blades, gears and pumps) and the cavitation noise of fluids travelling round a closed-loop internal system under pressure. The US Navy has gone to great lengths to reduce the internal noise of its SSNs: turbo-electric drive has been tried, thus dispensing with the need for steam turbines and noisy gear trains; and the S5G natural circulation reactor has been tested, doing away with reactor coolant pumps and the associated electrical and control equipment. These remain, however, one-off experiments.

Most submarines have only one propeller, although Soviet SSBNs and older SSNs have two. Propeller noise is generated mainly by tip-vortex cavitation, in which air-bubbles at the blade tips collapse with a hissing sound, radiating mostly in a horizontal plane in line with the blades. This noise increases with the momentum of the blades and is most pronounced at high speed, during acceleration and during manoeuvres. At lower speeds such propeller noise is modulated at the natural frequency of the blades them-selves to produce a characteristic 'beat', which is used for the identification of individual submarines. The use of two propellers accentuates these effects.

Magnetic Effects

A submarine hull is a large metal body which, when it moves, is cutting through the lines of force of the Earth's magnetic field. This creates a 'magnetic anomaly' which is detectable, especially by an airborne sensor. All advanced ASW aircraft are fitted with a Magnetic Anomaly Detector (MAD), which is not suitable for area search but is invaluable in locating precisely a target detected by other means. Submarines can also be detected by the electrical and magnetic fields they themselves create. There are electro-chemical processes on the hull of a submarine which generate varying electrical potentials, and an electric current flows between them, using sea water as the conductor. The rate of change of the resulting electrical and electro-magnetic fields can be discerned by very sensitive detectors such as large electric coils placed on the sea bed.

A submerged submarine leaves a wake, which can be detected by active sonar. Further, the turbulence eventually reaches the surface, where it causes tiny variations in the wave pattern which are detectable by Over-The-Horizon Backscatter (OTH-B) radar. The wake turbulence also forces cold water to rise and mix with the warmer surface water, thus causing a temperature differential which can be sensed by

Left: Lockheed S-3 Viking with its MAD 'sting' fully extended.

Right: USS *Sea Devil*, a Sturgeon class 'hunter-killer' SSN.

Above: West German Type 206 SSK running just below the surface. Conventional submarines must on occasion come up to 'breathe'.

satellite- or aircraft-mounted infra-red equipment. Moreover, when a submarine is moving at a shallow depth there is a very small but nevertheless perceptible rise in the surface of the water above the hull. This rise is potentially detectable by satellites such as the US SEASAT, which had a radio altimeter with a vertical resolution of 3·9in (10cm). The Soviet Union is particularly interested in this technique.

Communications

A particular problem is the need for submarines to communicate from time to time. The main means of communicating with a submerged submarine is by Very Low Frequency (VLF; 3–30KHz) radio, but external antennas are essential for reception. On patrol at its operating depth, for example, a US SSBN deploys a plastic buoy in which is embedded a crossed-loop antenna, whilst when moving at speed a wire antenna 1,673ft (510m) long must be streamed. Other communications systems require a submarine to rise to some 10ft (3m) below the surface, but Extra Low Frequency (ELF; 300Hz–3KHz) transmissions can be received at depths of 328ft (100m). In addition, to update its SINS an SSBN must expose a whip antenna above the surface for some 7–13 minutes. Not surprisingly, great efforts are being made to develop some new systems of communications and navigation which would overcome such dangerous ventures to the proximity of the surface.

SSNs are faster and more agile than SSBNs, but they, too, have a need to communicate with their bases from time to time. This was exemplified twice during the South Atlantic

13

War. During the build-up phase in early April 1982, Nimrod aircraft based on Ascension were 'involved as communications links for the transitting nuclear submarines' (*London Gazette,* Monday 13 December 1982), and later, on 2 May 1982, HMS *Conqueror* had to seek and then was granted authority to sink the cruiser *General Belgrano.* Any radio transmission is, of course, immediately detectable by enemy electronic surveillance, which will strive to analyse the content of the signal as well as pinpoint the site of the transmitter.

The SSK Problem

The major problem for SSKs is that they must routinely

Below: AN/SSQ-517 sonobuoy is a passive, air-deployed sensor.

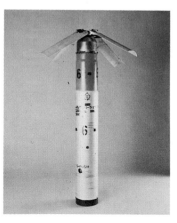

come up to the surface to obtain air to run their diesels and recharge their batteries. This can be achieved by only exposing the head of the schnorkel tube, but the latter is an easy target for modern radars and infra-red sensors. Further, the exhaust fumes from the schnorkel are detectable by 'sniffers' mounted on most ASW aircraft. Thus SSKs are faced with the contradiction that when submerged they are the quietest of all submarines and the most difficult to detect and on the other hand are inherently vulnerable due to this inescapable requirement to approach the surface at regular intervals.

Active Sonar

Active sonar devices transmit acoustic pulses in the audio frequency band which are reflected by a solid object such as a submarine. Pulse length and frequency are variable to suit the prevailing oceanic conditions. Range depends to a large extent upon transmission power, but the transfer of energy from the transducer to the ocean is a finite function which, if exceeded, results in cavitation and loss of power. This can only be overcome by enlarging the transmitting surface, which not only makes for complicated electronics but also can seriously affect the design of the ship. A further factor is

that the submarine can detect an active sonar transmitter earlier than the hunter can detect the target.

Passive Detection

The main passive acoustic detector is the hydrophone, a very sensitive listening device optimised for submarine noise. Hydrophones are deployed in static arrays on the ocean bed, on buoys, on the hulls of submarines, on the keels of surface ships (although here their effectiveness is limited at speed) and in sonobuoys. Both the USA and the Soviet Union deploy arrays of hydrophones positioned on the beds of the Pacific and Atlantic Oceans, but these do little more than establish the presence of submarines and their approximate directions; a follow-up platform such as an ASW aircraft is needed for pinpointing a target. The USA is now deploying the Surveillance Towed Array Sensor System (SURTASS), in which surface ships (civilian-manned) tow detection equipment along designated patrol lines, the resulting intelligence 'take' being passed in 'real time' via satellite links to two shore-based data processing centres. Towed arrays are now also being used by both surface warships and submarines, although arrays considerably smaller than SURTASS are involved.

The amount of information concerning ocean conditions and acoustic and other detections produced by all these means is simply enormous and has led to some extremely powerful computers; in several cases, advances in computer technology have been the result purely of pressure in the ASW field. Project 'Seaguard', for example, which integrates the US ASW 'take', led to the Illiac-4 computer, which comprises 64 normal computers in parallel, sharing a 10^9-bit bulk memory. The dramatic reduction in the size of computers has led to their installation in aircraft such as the Orion, Nimrod and Viking, but most ASW helicopters still have to pass sensor data back to their parent ship.

The Sub-Hunters

This book sets out to examine the more significant weapon and sensor platforms in this increasingly important strategic field. It cannot cover every single ship and aircraft, and omits those which have ASW only as a secondary function (for example, many modern destroyers and frigates). It must, however, be appreciated that primary ASW platforms do not operate alone—or only do so in unusual circumstances—but work as part of an integrated ASW team, combining to try to defeat their deadly enemy.

Surface Ships

There is a long-running controversy in most navies concerning the relative merits of surface ships and submarines as ASW platforms, and there can be little doubt that there are, indeed, certain aspects of the art in which submarines are superior. Nevertheless, surface ships can also perform certain functions for which a submarine is far less effective, including, for example, giving protection to task groups centred on a carrier, or to convoys against air and surface threats. Moreover —and in certain circumstances this can be very important indeed—surface warships can give a visible indication of a 'naval presence'.

Although most surface warships have at least some ASW capability, specialised ASW ships fall into three main categories. At the upper end are the aircraft carriers, such as *Kiev, Moskva, Invincible, Vittorio Veneto, Giuseppe Garibaldi* and *Príncipe de Asturias,* which have large flight decks and aircraft the majority of which are quite specifically intended for ASW. In the middle are the cruisers, destroyers and large frigates (the categories are somewhat flexible) epitomised by *Spruance, Udaloy, Broadsword, Kortenaer* and *Georges Leygues,* which are multiple-capability ships but in which the ASW role predominates. At the lower end are the very small frigates and corvettes, such as *D'Estienne d'Orves* and *Pauk,* in which, once again, ASW is the major of several functions.

The ASW carriers themselves cover a broad spectrum from 15,000 tons displacement to well over 42,000 tons. Having accepted the value of the helicopter as an ASW weapons system, these carriers represent a very effective means of providing them with an operating platform. This need not be at the expense of shipborne ASW weapons and sensors, although the heavy armament of the Soviet *Kiev* class is only obtained at the cost of considerable ship size.

For the medium-sized ASW ships, one of the crucial design criteria is whether the ship is to have one ASW helicopter or two. Two are obviously more effective in general, but a pair are essential if the ship is to carry out solo missions. Most of this category of surface ship have, in addition to their ASW sensors and weapons, a medium-calibre gun, anti-ship missiles, short/medium-range SAMs, and CIWS. In the smaller ships a helicopter is obviously impracticable, and they tend to concentrate, therefore, upon short-range weapons (torpedo-tubes and mortars) and sensors. Perhaps the finest in this category is the Soviet Navy's Pauk class corvette.

Above: HMS *Broadsword,* the first of the British Royal Navy's Type 22 frigates. Such surface warships seem to be the very epitome of naval might, but there is great debate about their efficacy as ASW platforms. The most important weapon in the ASW armoury of such ships is their ASW helicopter.

One of the great problems is that all too often operational requirements staffs and designers cannot resist the desire to put more and more systems into one multi-purpose hull, which leads inexorably to larger ships, greater complexity and larger crews—and escalating expense. Unless this tendency can be resisted many navies will find themselves able to afford fewer and fewer ships. One solution would appear to be to depart from the multi-purpose ship concept and return to specialisation, particularly for ASW missions. For the West, with a *Spruance* class destroyer costing $310 million (at 1981 prices) and a Type 22 costing £120 million (also at 1981 prices), something must be done to cut costs, otherwise there will not be the ships to keep the Soviet submarine threat under control.

Iroquois (DDH280) Class

Destroyers (Canada)

Four ships

Displacement: 3,551 tons standard; 4,700 tons full load.
Dimensions: Length overall 426ft (129·8m); beam 50ft (15·2m); draught 14·5ft (4·4m).
Propulsion: 2 Pratt & Whitney FT4A2 gas turbines, 50,000shp; 2 Pratt & Whitney FT12 AH3 gas turbines, 7,400shp; 2 shafts; 29kt.
Armament: 1 single 5in (127mm) OTO Melara Compact gun; 2 Sea Sparrow SAM launchers; 2 triple Mk 32 torpedo tubes; 1 triple Limbo ASW mortar.
Aircraft: 2 CHSS-2 Sea King.
ASW sensors: (Hull-mounted) SQS-505; (VDS) SQS-505.
Complement: 285.

The Royal Canadian Navy (RCN) has a wealth of experience of ASW operations in the North Atlantic stemming from its major contribution to the Allied effort in the Battle of the Atlantic during World War II. During the war and for some years afterwards the RCN relied upon British designs for its destroyers and frigates (albeit built in Canadian yards) but in 1951 it decided to design its own ships. The result has been a series of unusual-looking vessels, packed with innovations and well suited to their role in the frequently inhospitable environment of the northern seas.

First was the St Laurent class (2,260 tons), comprising six ships commissioned 1956-57. All underwent major refits in the 1970s but are due to be replaced by a new class in the late 1980s. Next into service was the Restigouche class (three ships), followed by the 'Improved Restigouche' class (four), the latter armed with Sea Sparrow SAMs, two 3in (76mm) guns and ASROC. The design was further developed into the Mackenzie class (four ships) and the Annapolis class (two), which were commissioned in 1962-64.

Right: HMCS *Iroquois* (DDH280) nameship of her class (left) with HMCS *Nipigon* (DDH266) of the Annapolis class alongside. Canadian destroyer designs are instantly recognisable, their apparently idiosyncratic features the result of long experience of operating in northern Atlantic waters.

Below: HMCS *Huron* (DDH281) of the DDH280 class. The large hangar houses two CHSS-2 Sea King ASW helicopters, one of which is seen on the flight-deck. Also visible is the stern-mounted SQS-505 VDS with its 18ft (5·48m) towed body stowed.

In the early 1970s the DDH280 class (*Iroquois, Huron, Athabaskan, Algonquin*) appeared. These have a distinctive appearance with a high bridge and hangar, surmounted by a lattice mast and bifurcated funnel. The RCN has always used large helicopters in relation to the size of its hulls, and the DDH280s carry two CHSS-2 Sea Kings. Landing is assisted by the 'Beartrap', a Canadian-invented cable device which is attached to the hovering helicopter and which then hauls the aircraft down on to the deck. ASW sensors include a hull-mounted SQS-505 sonar in a 14ft (4·26m) dome and an SQS-505 variable-depth sonar, which is streamed from the stern. ASW weapons include the Mk 10 Limbo mortar and two triple Mk 32 torpedo tubes firing Mk 46 torpedoes.

The next class of destroyers is awaited with considerable interest, as the Canadian designers will doubtless have a few more surprises for the naval world. Six ships have been ordered, each equipped with one Sea King helicopter and displacing less than 4,000 tons. Total cost for the class is estimated to be £2·3 billion.

Clémenceau Class

Aircraft carriers (France)

Two ships

Displacement: 27,307 tons standard; 32,780 tons full load.
Dimensions: Length overall 870ft (265m); beam 168ft (51·2m); draught 28·1ft (8·6m).
Propulsion: Geared steam turbines, 126,000shp; 2 shafts; 32kt.
Armament: 8 single 3·9in (100mm) DP guns.
Aircraft: 16 Super Étendard; 3 Étendard IVP; 7 Breguet Alizé; 2 Aérospatiale Alouette III.
ASW sensors: (Hull-mounted) SQS-503.
Complement: 1,338.

Clémenceau and *Foch* were commissioned in the early 1960s and incorporated all the major advances made in carrier operating techniques during the immediate postwar period. The flight deck is angled at 8° to the ship's major axis. The forward aircraft lift is offset to starboard and the after lift is positioned on the deck-edge to clear the flight deck and to increase hangar capacity.

The attack aircraft is the Dassault Super Étendard, which can carry anti-ship (ASM) missiles such as the Exocet, as was demonstrated so dramatically by the Argentine naval air arm during the South Atlantic war in 1982. The small size and light construction of the ships, together with the limited capacity of their lifts and catapults, have made it difficult to find a replacement for the Crusader fighter aircraft formerly carried. The ASW aircraft is the Breguet Alizé; ten are carried, but these are now somewhat aged, although no replacement is in sight. A further limitation on the effectiveness of these ships is the lack of an integral airborne early warning (AEW) aircraft, and a French carrier group would thus suffer the same problems as the Royal Navy task force experienced in the South Atlantic in 1982.

The French Navy plans to replace these two aircraft carriers with new nuclear-powered carriers in the 1990s. These will be enormously expensive for such a relatively small navy and will take up a disproportionate amount of the available resources, but they will nevertheless be a valuable addition to NATO's maritime capabilities.

Below: Two Super Frelon ASW helicopters on the deck of *Foch*.

D'Estienne d'Orves Class

Frigates (France)

Sixteen ships + 1 building

Displacement: 950 tons standard; 1,250 tons full load.
Dimensions: Length overall 262·5ft (80m); beam 33·8ft (10·3m); draught 9·8ft (3m).
Propulsion: 2 SEMT-Pielstick diesels, 11,000bhp; 2 shafts; 24kt.
Armament: 1 3·9in (100mm) gun; 2 20mm guns; all ships fitted for 2 Exocet SSM launchers but only those deployed overseas will mount missiles; 1 375mm rocket launcher; 4 fixed torpedo tubes.
Aircraft: None.
ASW sensors: (Hull-mounted) DUBA-25.
Complement: 79.

Above: *D'Estienne d'Orves* with Exocet launchers beside funnel.

Above: *Drogou* (F-738), 1,250 tons full load, in the Mediterranean.

The D'Estienne d'Orves class are small, specialised vessels with a very limited air defence armament and are primarily intended for ASW operations in coastal waters, although they are also used for overseas deployments in French colonial waters. In the French Navy they are designated 'avisos'.

The sonar is the Thomson-CSF Tarpon DUBA-25, an active sonar in a hull mounting, which provides all-round surveillance, target acquisition and attack facilities for these small ships. ASW weapons are one 375mm Mk 54 rocket launcher and four fixed tubes for L3 or L5 torpedoes. The single 3·9in (100mm) gun is mounted forward, just ahead of the bridge, and those ships deployed overseas also mount two MM.38 Exocets, one on either side of the funnel. Two 20mm AA guns are also fitted.

The seventeenth and last of this neat design is already under construction. The next class to be built is the 'Aviso Deuxième Génération', which will carry a towed sonar array and will be in the 2,000-ton class. These 'avisos' are approximately the same size as the larger 'corvettes' of World War II, but it would appear that the French Navy has tried to put too much into a 1,250-ton hull, and this is tacitly admitted by the increase in the next generation to 2,000 tons. Perhaps it would have been better with this class to have concentrated on the ASW role rather than to try to make them into 'mini-frigates' by adding so much other weaponry.

Georges Leygues (C70) Class

Destroyers (France)
Four ships + 4 building

Displacement: 3,380 tons standard; 4,170 tons full load.
Dimensions: Length overall 455·9ft (139m); beam 45·9ft (14m); draught 18·7ft (5·7m).
Propulsion: 2 Rolls-Royce Olympus gas turbines, 52,000shp; 2 SEMT-Pielstick diesels, 10,400bhp; 2 shafts; 30kt.
Armament: 1 3·9in (100mm) gun; 2 20mm guns; 2 torpedo tubes.
Aircraft: 1 WG13 Lynx.
ASW sensors: (Hull-mounted) DUBV-23; (VDS) DUBV-43.
Complement: 226.

Right: *Montcalm* (D-642). In the second batch of four ships the bridge will be raised by one deck level, as the current design has proved too low, especially with sea breaking over the forecastle.

Below: Nameship of the class, *Georges Leygues* (D-640), at sea. Launched in 1974 and commissioned in 1979 she now serves with the Mediterranean Fleet. The basic hull design is being used for eight ASW ships and for another two equipped for the AA role.

The French Navy has produced a very efficient hull design for the C70 ships which are being produced in two versions—the basic C70 (Georges Leygues) class for ASW, and the C70AA (AA = 'anti-airienne') for air defence. Current plans envisage eight of the ASW version and four of the AA, but further orders might well be forthcoming. The first of the class, *Georges Leygues,* was commissioned on 10 December 1979 and four are now with the fleet; the remaining four will be commissioned at a rate of one per year over the period 1985–88. Although these ships are officially classified as 'corvettes' by the French Navy, they have been given 'D' pennant numbers and would, in fact, be counted as destroyers by any other navy.

The principal ASW sensors are the bow-mounted, low-frequency DUBV-23 sonar and the very closely related DUBV-43 variable-depth sonar. The DUBV-23 array is mounted in a streamlined bulb and performs both search and attack functions. In the DUBV-43 the transducer array is mounted in a 'fish' which is streamed over the stern at distances of up to 820ft (250m) and at depths ranging from 33ft (10m) to 656ft (200m). Virtually all elements of the two systems are identical apart from the transducer arrays, and even they consist of essentially similar components. The main shipborne ASW weapon is the L5 torpedo, of which ten are mounted in fixed launchers. The L5 is an electric-powered 21in (533mm) weapon with an active/passive head and a speed of 35k. The other main element of the C70's ASW capability is the two WG13 Lynx helicopter (qv) which have identical airframes with the British version but are fitted with French avionics and sensors. Other weapons include four Exocet launchers (a further four can be added in war) and 26 Crotale SAMs. There is also one 3·9in (100mm) gun in a DP mounting on the foredeck.

The second batch of four ships is expected to have a number of improvements. Visually, the most noticeable change will be the raising of the bridge by one deck level as the current position (low and rather far forward) has proved unsuitable in bad weather, especially with seas breaking over the bow. The ships will also carry a new sonar, the SS-48, a very sophisticated bow-mounted VDS system which has been some ten years in development. This will be fitted in the fifth and subsequent ships during construction, and will be retrofitted to the earlier four during mid-life refits. It is also hoped to install the new Vampir long-range infra-red surveillance sensor, as well as a new version of the Crotale SAM missile with an additional sea-skimming anti-ship capability.

Giuseppe Garibaldi Class

Aircraft carrier (Italy)

One ship

Displacement: 10,100 tons standard; 13,370 tons full load.
Dimensions: Length overall 591ft (180·1m); beam 100ft (30·5m); draught 22ft (6·7m).
Propulsion: COGAG; 4 LM2500 gas turbines, 80,000shp; 2 shafts; 30kt.
Armament: 4 Otomat Mk 2 SSM launchers; 2 octuple Albatros SAM systems; 3 twin Breda 40mm guns; 2 triple Mk 32 torpedo tubes.
Aircraft: 18 SH-3D Sea King.
ASW sensors: (Hull-mounted) DE-1160.
Complement: 550.

Following a series of helicopter-carrying cruisers, the Italian Navy has finally decided to produce a full-blown aircraft-carrier, although the project has been a far from easy one and there may be further problems ahead. Nevertheless, *Giuseppe Garibaldi* was launched on 4 June 1943 and is scheduled to join the fleet in 1985. She is designed for ASW operations and will carry eighteen SH-3D Sea King helicopters in place of the AB 204/212s which serve aboard earlier ships. The hangar, which is located centrally, is 361ft (110m) long and 20ft (6m) high, with a maximum width of 49ft (15m). Twelve Sea Kings can be struck down in the hangar, which is divided into three sections by fire curtains, but the other aircraft must remain on the flight deck. Six helicopter spots are marked on the deck.

Right: *Giuseppe Garibaldi* (C-551) immediately after launch on 4 June 1983. The neat lines of the design are clearly visible as is the 6° 'ski-jump'. It is still not clear, however, whether the Italian Navy will be allowed to operate V/STOL aircraft.

Below: A model of *Giuseppe Garibaldi* with six of the planned eighteen SH-3D Sea King ASW helicopters on deck. The culmination of a long line of development by the Italian Navy, *Garibaldi* is a prime example of the growing number of light (10-20,000 tons) helicopter carriers designed for the important ASW role.

Short-range air defence and close-in anti-missile systems are fitted, and these are all of Italian design and manufacture, as are the Selenia surveillance, 3-D tracking and fire control radars. A bow sonar is fitted; this is a Raytheon DE-1167, manufactured in Italy under licence by Elsag.

Giuseppe Garibaldi's most striking feature is a 91ft (28m) 6° ski-jump, which has no feasible helicopter application and is quite clearly intended for use by Sea Harrier V/STOL aircraft. This whole problem has been the subject of a major interservice row between the Italian Navy and Air Force: the Navy desperately wants fixed-wing aircraft at sea but is not allowed to operate them, while the Air Force is adamant in its refusal to provide a sea-going component. There the matter rests for the moment, but meanwhile the Italian Navy has built itself a very useful light aircraft carrier, optimised for the ASW role. The design makes an interesting comparison with the Spanish *Príncipe de Asturias* (page 47).

Vittorio Veneto Class

Cruiser (Italy)

One ship

Displacement: 7,500 tons standard; 8,850 tons full load.
Dimensions: Length overall 589ft (179·5m); beam 64ft (19·5m); draught 20ft (6m).
Propulsion: Geared steam turbines, 73,000shp; 2 shafts; 32kt.
Armament: 1 twin Mk 10 launcher (60 Terrier/ASROC missiles); 8 single 3in (76mm) DP guns; 2 triple Mk 32 torpedo tubes.
Aircraft: 9 AB 212 or 4 SH-3D Sea King.
ASW sensors: (Hull-mounted) SQS-23.
Complement: 550.

Above: *Vittorio Veneto* **(C-550), current flagship of the Commander-in-Chief of the Italian Fleet. Note the relatively heavy armament and general similarity to the Soviet Moskva class.**

Vittorio Veneto is the third in a series of Italian air-capable ASW cruisers completed in the 1960s; *Andrea Doria* and *Caio Duilio* are smaller and operate only four AB204 ASW helicopters with a conventional large double hangar. In *Vittorio Veneto* these arrangements are much modified: there is an extra deck aft with a large hangar beneath it; and there are four helicopter spots on the capacious flight-deck, which is served by a large centreline lift. *Vittorio Veneto* was designed to operate nine AB 204 helicopters, but these have now been superseded by the AB 212 (qv), with an alternative complement of four Sea Kings.

In a recently completed refit, *Vittorio Veneto*'s armament was revised: the Terrier missile system was upgraded to fire the Standard SM-1 (ER) missile, and the single 76mm was replaced by three twin 40mm/70 Breda compact mountings with Dardo fire control systems; four Otomat Mk2 SSMs were also fitted. On-board ASW equipment remains a hull-mounted SQS-23 sonar and two triple Mk 32 torpedo tubes firing Mk 46 torpedoes.

Vittorio Veneto is a handsome and effective warship, and well suited for the prime role of ASW in a Mediterranean environment. Like the *Andrea Doria* class, she lacks a powerful surface weapon, but, like them, she is designed to operate as part of a task force.

Maestrale Class

Frigates (Italy)
Eight ships

Displacement: 2,500 tons standard; 3040 tons full load.
Dimensions: Length overall 405ft (122·7m); beam 42·5ft (12·9m); draught (screws) 27·4ft (8·4m).
Propulsion: 2 Fiat gas turbines, 50,000shp; 2 diesels, 11,000bhp; 2 shafts; 32kt.
Armament: 4 Otomat Mk 2 SSM launchers; 1 5in (127mm) gun; 4 40mm guns; 2 triple Mk 32 torpedo tubes.
Aircraft: None.
ASW sensors: (Hull-mounted) DE-1164.
Complement: 232.

In the 1970s the Italian Navy built a successful class of 2,500-ton convoy escort frigates of the Lupo class. These have a respectable ASW armament of two triple Mk 32 torpedo tubes and a hangar for an ASW helicopter. Four were built for Italy and there have been a number of export orders: Iraq (4), Peru (4) and Venezuela (6). The Maestrale class, now under construction, has a superficial similarity to the Lupos but is, in fact, a new design to meet a new and different operational requirement for a fleet ASW escort. Obviously, however, the experience gained with the Lupos has been put to good effect in the new class.

ASW armament for *Maestrale* comprises two triple Mk 32 torpedo tubes for Mk 46 torpedoes, plus two fixed launchers for Whitehead Moto Fides A184 wire-guided torpedoes. The principal ASW sensor is the Raytheon DE-1164 integrated hull-mounted and variable-depth sonar. Finally, there is a flight deck and hangar for either one SH-3 Sea King or two AB 212 ASW helicopters. Surface armament comprises four Otomat Mk 2 SSMs and one 5in (127mm) gun in a DP mounting; air defence armament includes four 40mm automatic cannon and an Albatros launcher with eight Aspide SAMs.

Eight Maestrales have so far been ordered, all for the Italian Navy. The first was commissioned in February 1982 and the eighth will join the fleet in 1984.

Below: The Italian Navy's frigate *Maestrale* (F-570) at speed in the Tyrrhenian Sea. Eight of this class have been ordered, the last being due to join the fleet during 1984.

Shirane/Haruna Classes

Destroyers (Japan)

Two/two ships

Displacement: 5,200 tons standard; 6,800 tons full load.
Dimensions: Length overall 521ft (158·8m); beam 57·5ft (17·5m); draught 17·5ft (5·3m).
Propulsion: Geared steam turbines, 70,000shp; 2 shafts; 32kt.
Armament: 1 octuple ASROC Mk 16 launcher; 2 single 5in (127mm) Mk 42 guns; 1 Sea Sparrow SAM launcher; 2 Phalanx CIWS; 2 triple Mk 32 torpedo tubes.
Aircraft: 3 SH-3B Sea King.
ASW sensors: (Hull-mounted) OQS-101; (VDS) SQS-35 (J).
Complement: 350.
(Specifications given for Shirane class; see text for details of Haruna class.)

The Soviet Pacific Fleet is based at Vladivostok, Sovetskaya Gavan and Petropavlovsk-Kamchatskiy, none of which have direct access to the ocean. It is Japan's misfortune to sit astride most of the exits, as well as being the only non-Soviet navy with access to the Sea of Okhotsk. Mindful of the large submarine component of the Soviet Navy, the Japanese Maritime Self-Defence Force (JMSDF) has built up a naval element with a primary ASW role. Its surface ships are of Japanese design and construction, but tend to use weapons systems and armament of US origin, either locally

Below: The Japanese MSDF has built up a useful ASW force of surface ships, the latest class being the Shirane, with the nameship of the class (DD-143) shown here. An SH-3B Sea King is landing on.

manufactured under licence or purchased directly. The showpieces of the fleet are the four helicopter-carrying ASW destroyers of the Haruna and Shirane classes; the former were completed in 1973–74 and the latter in 1980–81.

Both classes have a very large hangar which accommodates three Mitsubishi SH-3B (licence-built Sikorsky Sea King) helicopters. The spacious flight deck extends to the stern, and incorporates the Canadian 'Beartrap' haul-down system. Both classes have an ASROC launcher forward of the bridge and Mk 64 torpedo tubes in two triple mountings abreast the bridge. Hull sonars of Japanese design and manufacture are fitted (OQS-3 in *Haruna;* OQS-101 in *Shirane). Shirane* currently is the only class to have SQS-35 VDS, but this will be fitted to the earlier pair at their next refit. The Shiranes also have SQR-18 TACTASS towed arrays. Surface armament includes two quick-firing 5in (127mm) Mk 42 guns in all four ships, complemented by BPDMS and Phalanx CIWS in the Shirane class. The *Harunas* are to be fitted with Sea Sparrow at their next refit.

These are two classes of impressive and capable ships, in the best Japanese maritime traditions. The JMSDF will soon have a surface fleet of 35 destroyers and 18 frigates, all optimised for the ASW role.

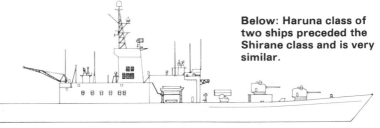

Below: Haruna class of two ships preceded the Shirane class and is very similar.

Tromp Class

Destroyers (Netherlands)

Two ships

Displacement: 3,900 tons standard; 4,580 tons full load.
Dimensions: Length overall 454·1ft (138·4m); beam 48·6ft (14·8m); draught 15·1ft (4·6m).
Propulsion: 2 Rolls-Royce Olympus gas turbines, 50,000shp; 2 Rolls-Royce Tyne cruising gas turbines, 8,000shp; 2 shafts; 30kt.
Armament: 8 Harpoon SSM launchers; 1 Tartar Mk 13 SAM launcher; 2 quadruple Sea Sparrow SAM launchers; 1 twin 4·7in (120mm) gun; 2 triple Mk 32 torpedo tubes.
Aircraft: 1 WG13 Lynx.
ASW sensors: (Hull-mounted) CWE-610.
Complement: 246.

It is the Dutch intention to create an integrated, efficient and balanced fleet, at the heart of which will be three task forces each comprising a flagship, six ASW frigates and a logistic support vessel. Two of these forces will be allocated to CINCEASTLANT and one to CINCHAN. Two of the three flagships will be *Tromp* and *De Ruyter*, one of the finest designs of recent years. Their armament is particularly heavy, with a twin 4·7in (120mm) turret, Sea Sparrow BPDMS, Standard Tartar SAM and Harpoon SSMs. Two of the major visual features are the high bridge, surmounted by the enormous Hollandse Signaalapparat radome, and the bifurcated uptakes. Triple Mk 32 torpedo tubes are mounted either side of the after superstructure, firing Mk 46 torpedoes. Refits for these two ships are planned for 1984–86.

The remaining ships in the three Dutch task forces, apart from the Kortenaers described below, will be six frigates of the Van Speijk class. These are Dutch-built, somewhat modified versions of the British Leander class; all have recently completed mid-life refits and will continue to serve for the foreseeable future.

The Tromp class represent the upper end of the type of all-round destroyer/frigate which the smaller navies can afford to build. The success of the Dutch concepts was not, however, to come with the Tromps, good as they are, but with the next class, which incorporates all the lessons learned—the Kortenaers.

Below: The unmistakable profile of a Tromp class frigate. The huge radome houses a Hollandse Signaalapparat 3-dimensional radar antenna. Designed as flagships for the Dutch task forces operating under NATO command in war, these two ships represent one of the most outstanding postwar surface warship designs.

Kortenaer Class

Frigates (Netherlands)

Twelve ships + two air defence version + 13 ordered

Displacement: 3,050 tons standard; 3,630 tons full load.
Dimensions: Length overall 428ft (130m), beam 47·2ft (14·4m); draught 14·3ft (4·4m).
Propulsion: 2 Rolls-Royce Olympus gas turbines, 50,000shp; 2 Rolls-Royce Olympus gas turbines, 8,000shp; 2 shafts; 30kt.
Armament: 1 quadruple Harpoon SSM launcher; 1 octuple Sea Sparrow SAM launcher; 2 single 3in (76mm) guns; 2 twin Mk 32 torpedo tubes.
Aircraft: 2 WG13 Lynx.
ASW sensors: (Hull-mounted) SQS-505.
Complement: 167.

The balance of the ships for the three Dutch task groups referred to in the *Tromp* entry above will come from the Kortenaer class. Following failure to agree on the specification for the successor to the Leander class (*Van Speijk* in Dutch service) the British and the Dutch decided to go their separate ways. The result for the Dutch Navy is the Kortenaer class (of which twelve have so far been ordered, the last two being laid down as flagships), with extra air defences and without the hangar, although the flight-deck is being retained. The ASW fit includes a bow-mounted SQS-505 sonar, two Lynx helicopters (only one is normally carried in peacetime) and two twin Mk 32 torpedo tubes for Mk 46 torpedoes.

The West German Navy has ordered six ships of a modified Kortenaer design to replace the old ships of the Köln and Fletcher classes. These ships (the Bremen class) are intended for ASW missions in the Baltic, and all six will have been commissioned by the end of 1984. The Greek Navy has ordered four, with the possibility of a fifth to follow later; the first two units of the Elli class were built in Holland, but the second pair will be built locally in the Hellenic Shipyards at Scaramanga. Portugal has also confirmed an order for three ships. Thus, with firm orders for 27 of these well-designed, well-equipped and highly respected ships already received, the Dutch are justified in their belief that they have produced a 'winner', which has more claim than most to being the NATO 'standard frigate'.

Below: Hr Ms *Kortenaer* (F-807), nameship of a class of twelve for the Dutch Navy, with a further thirteen on order for other NATO navies. With a weapons and sensor fit optimised for ASW these ships are intended for deep ocean operations and will provide the main part of the three Dutch task forces, together with the two Tromp and six Van Speijk class frigates. Note the large flight-deck and spacious hangar for the two Lynx ASW helicopters.

Kiev Class

ASW aircraft carriers (Soviet Union)

Four ships

Displacement: 36,000 tons standard; 42,000 tons full load.
Dimensions: Length overall 899ft (274m); beam 157·5ft (48m); draught 33ft (10m).
Propulsion: Geared steam turbines, 180,000shp; 4 shafts; 32kt.
Armament: 8 SS-N-12 launchers; 2 twin SA-N-3 launchers; 2 twin SA-N-4 launchers; 2 twin 3in (76·2mm) DP guns; 8 30mm Gatling CIWS; 1 twin SUW-N-1 launcher; 2 RBU 6000 launchers; 2 quintuple 21in (533mm) torpedo tubes.
Aircraft: 12 Yak-36MP Forger; 18–21 Ka-25 Hormone-A/B.
ASW sensors: (Hull-mounted) LF sonar; (VDS) MF sonar.
Complement: 2,500.

The primary role of these splendid warships is ASW, and for this they carry two squadrons of 15–18 Kamov Ka-25 Hormone-A helicopters, an SUW-N-1 launcher forward and the usual complement of ASW mortars and torpedo tubes. Principal shipborne ASW sensors are a low-fequency sonar mounted in the bow, and a variable-depth sonar streamed from the stern.

The principal air defence system, the SA-N-3, is the same as on the Moskvas, but the layout of the Kievs' launchers—one forward and one aft of the bridge island—is obviously more satisfactory. The other major air defence weapons are similarly deployed: a twin 76mm gun mounting on the forecastle and a second on the after end of the superstructure; an SA-N-4 'bin' on the port side of the forecastle and another on the starboard side of the island; and groups of paired Gatling CIWS at each of the four quadrants.

The long, narrow hangar accommodates the two squadrons of helicopters and a squadron of Yakovlev Yak-36 Forger VTOL aircraft. The flight deck is angled at 4° but does not have the 'ski-jump' which has made such a difference to the performance of the Sea Harriers on the British Invincible class ships, probably because the Forger cannot currently perform rolling short take-offs.

Kiev and *Novorosiiysk* are deployed with the Northern Fleet and *Minsk* with the Pacific Fleet; the fourth of class will probably join the latter when she completes her sea trials later in 1984. In the event of hostilities the Kievs would probably be employed in support of Soviet submarines in their respective areas, against NATO submarine and surface threats. This could involve the protection of the SSBN bastions in the Barents Sea in the west and in the Sea of Okhotsk in the east, and also offensive forays against NATO ASW barrier forces in such critical areas as the GIUK gap.

It is expected that this class will be completed by the fourth ship now on trials. It can only be assumed that the Soviet Navy's next step will be a nuclear-powered aircraft carrier. Having seen the way in which the Soviet naval architects manage to surprise their Western counterparts so often, there is no telling what the new ships may look like.

Above: *Kiev* at sea
with her heavy
weapons fit clearly
visible on the
forecastle, together
with eight Ka-25
Hormone ASW heli-
copters and two Yak-
36 Forgers. The Gatlings
can also be seen.

Right: *Kiev*, name ship
of the class of four at
sea. Door in stern is
for a Variable-Depth
Sonar (VDS) ASW
sensor.

Left: Kiev class carrier
at speed. Western
experts assess that
only four of this class
will be built, and that
the next Soviet Navy
carriers will be
nuclear-powered
ships of 60,000 tons,
which will pose a major
threat to the West.

Moskva Class

ASW helicopter cruisers (Soviet Union)

Two ships

Displacement: 16,500 tons standard; 20,000 tons full load.
Dimensions: Length overall 625ft (190·5m); beam 112ft (34m); draught 25ft (7·6m).
Propulsion: Geared steam turbines, 100,000shp; 2 shafts; 30kt.
Armament: 2 twin SA-N-3 launchers; 2 twin 57mm guns; 1 twin SUW-N-1 launcher; 2 RBU 6000 launchers.
Aircraft: 18 Ka-25 Hormone-A.
ASW sensors: (Hull-mounted) LF sonar; (VDS) MF sonar.
Complement: 850.

Right: *Moskva* ASW cruiser in the Mediterranean. The heavy armament on the
forecastle can be seen as can the concentration of sensors on the pyramid-shaped
superstructure. The flight-deck is 265·7 ×
111·5ft (81 × 34m) in size, with four helicopter
spots; Yak-36 Forger VTOL aircraft
cannot, however, operate from this class.

Below: Two Ka-25 Hormone ASW helicopters
sit with their rotor blades folded on the
flight-deck of a Moskva class cruiser. Gun
abreast the funnel is a twin 57mm dual-
purpose mounting, one of two fitted.

Above: An overhead view of *Moskva* with the two narrow lifts, which are restricted to Hormones, clearly visible on the flight-deck.

Designated 'protivolodochny kreyser' (anti-submarine cruiser) by the Soviet Navy, *Moskva* first appeared in 1967 and served notice on the West that the Russians were moving into the shipborne aviation business in a big way. There is no doubt that these two well-designed ships were intended primarily to hunt US Navy SSBNs in the eastern Mediterranean, but they also served to train Soviet Navy ships' crews and aviators in operating large numbers of aircraft at sea. They were thus, to a large degree, stepping-stones on the way to the Kiev class.

The design of the Moskvas may have been influenced to a certain extent by the helicopter cruisers built for the French and Italian Navies in the early 1960s, but the Soviet design is much larger, able to operate an air group of 15–18 Kamov Ka-25 Hormones housed in a spacious hangar beneath the half-length flight deck. This is served by two aircraft lifts, which are somewhat narrow and limit the ship to Hormones; even the Mil Mi-8 Hip is too large to use them.

The primary ASW weapons system of the Moskvas is the Ka-25 helicopters, which are normally of the ASW Hormone-A type (qv) although some of the -B version may also be carried. Unlike Western aircraft carriers, however, the forward part of the Soviet ships is occupied by a comprehensive outfit of ASW and air defence systems. ASW sensors include a hull-mounted low-frequency sonar and a variable-depth sonar trailed from the stern. There is a twin SUW-N-1 anti-submarine missile launcher on the forecastle, and two RBU 6000 twelve-barrelled rocket launchers on the bow. There is also an SA-N-3 area air defence system, and two twin 57mm dual-purpose gun mountings seem to have been fitted almost as an afterthought. The tall, pyramid-shaped superstructure includes the bridge, the funnel and the numerous radio, radar and ESM antennas found on all Soviet warships.

Only two units of the class were built, *Moskva* and *Leningrad*, and they have served the Soviet Navy well, although Soviet interest in medium-sized air-capable ships appears now to have waned in favour of the very much larger ships of the Kiev class.

Udaloy Class

Cruisers (Soviet Union)

Six ships

Displacement: 6,500 tons standard; 8,000 tons full load.
Dimensions: Length overall 531·4ft (162m); beam 59ft (18m); draught 20ft (6m).
Propulsion: 2 gas turbines, 30,000shp; 2 gas turbines, 6,000shp; 35kt.
Armament: 2 quadruple SS-N-14 launchers; 2 RBU 6000 launchers; 8 VLS canisters for SA-N-?; 2 3·9in (100mm) guns; 4 30mm Gatling guns; 2 quintuple 21in (533mm) torpedo tubes.
Aircraft: 2 Ka-25 Hormone-A (Ka-27 Helix-A can be carried).
ASW sensors: (Hull-mounted) LF sonar; (VDS) MF sonar.
Complement: 350.

The *Udaloy* is of great interest because it is optimised for the ASW role and is clearly intended to be the anti-submarine component of a mixed battle group operating at some distance from its base, probably in the northern and central Atlantic. The ASW armament is exceptionally powerful. There are the now standard quadruple SS-N-14 launchers abreast the bridge, two RBU 6000 rocket launchers, and two quadruple 21in (533mm) torpedo tubes amidships. *Udaloy* has two separate hangars for its pair of Hormone-A ASW helicopters, the first Soviet cruiser or destroyer to be equipped to operate two rather than one aircraft. The landing platform is large and located above the VDS well on the stern, but the hangar floor is one deck

lower with a ramp for moving the aircraft from one level to the other. The sharp rake of the bow suggests a large low-frequency sonar dome fitted below, and this tends to be confirmed by the characteristics of the bow wave. There is a VDS at the stern, streamed over the transom in line with Soviet naval practice.

Other weapons are somewhat limited. There are two 100mm dual-purpose guns in single mountings in the 'A' and 'B' positions, together with four 30mm Gatling CIWS. Air defence is provided by eight SAM launchers, of an unidentified type. Air and surface surveillance radars are also rather limited by previous Soviet standards.

In view of the similarity in dimensions and displacement between this class and the Sovremenny class, which appeared at the same time but are optimised for the anti-surface role, it is surprising that the two classes do not share a common hull. This certainly would have been the case for a Western navy, but the political and economic constraints upon the Soviet Navy are much less severe and they have been permitted to optimise the hull form as well. The propulsion method is also different, *Sovremenny* having steam turbines and *Udaloy* gas turbines (which are particularly suited for the ASW mission).

These ships are classified by the Soviets as *'bol'shoy protivolodochny korable'* (large ASW ship, BPK) and by NATO as DDGs, although their size suggests that the designation 'cruiser' is much more appropriate. Six vessels of this very capable and interesting class are in service, and many more can be expected to follow.

Below: Udaloy class cruiser; note flight-deck and helicopter hangar.

Kara Class

Cruisers (Soviet Union)
Seven ships

Displacement: 8,200 tons standard; 1,000 tons full load.
Dimensions: Length overall 568 ft (173·2m); beam 59ft (18m); draught 22ft (6·7m).
Propulsion: COGAG; 100,000shp; 2 shafts; 32kt.
Armament: 2 quadruple SS-N-14 launchers; 2 RBU 6000 and 2 RBU 1000 launchers; 2 twin SA-N-4 launchers; 2 twin SA-N-3 launchers; 2 twin 3in (76mm) guns; 4 30mm Gatling guns; 2 quintuple 21in (533mm) torpedo tubes.
Aircraft: 1 Ka-25 Hormone-A.
ASW sensors: (Hull-mounted) LF sonar; (VDS) MF sonar.
Complement: 540.

The Kara class is a development of the Kresta-II. Gas turbine propulsion has been adopted in place of steam, leading to major changes in the layout of the midships section. Uptakes for the four large gas turbines are led up to a single, huge, square funnel, a major characteristic of the class. The Head Net-C surveillance radar antenna has been moved forward to a lattice mast on top of the large bridge to carry it clear of the hot exhausts.

Compared to the Kresta-II, a 50ft (15m) section has been added between the bridge and the tower mast to accommodate a larger calibre gun (76mm as opposed to 57mm) and the SA-N-4 close-range surface-to-air missile. Cylindrical bins for the latter are mounted on either side of the tower mast, with the adjacent Pop Group guidance radar antennas protected by high, curved blast screens. The close-in anti-missile Gatlings are abreast the funnel. One consequence of this concentration of armament in the waist of the ship is a blind arc of a full 50° aft and 20° forward for the SA-N-4 launchers, although since these missiles manoeuvre after launch this is probably not especially critical.

The ASW fit is comprehensive. There are eight SS-N-14 ASW missiles in two quadruple launch bins on either side of the bridge; there are also two 12-barrel RBU 6000 launchers on the forecastle and a further two 6-barrel RBU 1000s beside the hangar aft. There is a large bow-mounted sonar and

Below: The electronics and weapons fit of a Kara class cruiser is typical of the complexity of a modern warship. Fitting all these into a hull of limited size involves many compromises, although Soviet designers seem particularly skilled in this art.

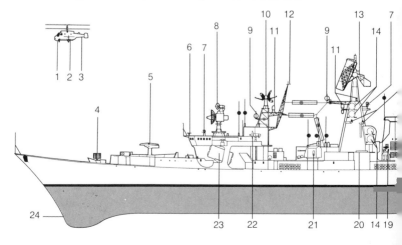

a variable-depth sonar in the stern. One Kamov Ka-25 Hormone-A ASW helicopter is carried; there is a fair-sized landing platform on the stern (above the VDS well) and a hangar with a ramp leading to the next lower deck.

The size of the bridge structure—wider, a deck higher and almost twice as long as on the *Kara*—indicates a major increase in the space available for command and control functions, but Kara deployments to date do not suggest a flagship role. Two are with the Pacific Fleet, but the remainder of the class serves in the Mediterranean and Black Seas. Production of the Karas ended in 1976, and the facilities at the Zhdanov Yard in Leningrad are now devoted to the cruiser originally designated by NATO as 'BLACKCOM 1' but now known to be the Krasina class.

Below: Kara class cruiser about to replenish from a Kazbek class fleet oiler. The landing pad and hangar for the Ka-25 are aft, and the housing for the VDS can be seen on the stern.

(1)	Radar.	(7)	Don Kay radar.	(13)	Top Sail radar.
(2)	Dunking sonar.	(8)	Headlight Group B	(14)	Side Globe ESM
(3)	MAD.		fire control system.		antenna.
(4)	Anti-submarine	(9)	Cross loop HF/DF.	(15)	Bass Tilt radar.
	rocket launcher.	(10)	Head Net C radars.	(16)	Variable depth sonar.
(5)	SA-N-3 launcher.	(11)	Bell ECM.	(17)	Torpedo tubes.
(6)	Don-2 radar.	(12)	High Pole IFF.	(18)	Close-in weapon
					system.
				(19)	Pop Group fire
					control system.
				(20)	SA-N-4 launcher.
				(21)	Twin 76mm gun.
				(22)	Owl Screech fire
					control radar.
				(23)	SS-N-14 launcher.
				(24)	Hull-mounted sonar.

- HF whip aerials
- Wire antennae (communications)

Kresta-II Class

Cruisers (Soviet Union)

Ten ships

Displacement: 6,000 tons standard; 7,800 tons full load.
Dimensions: Length overall 519·9ft (158·5m); beam 55·4ft (17m); draught: 19·7ft (6m).
Propulsion: Geared steam turbines, 100,000shp; 2 shafts; 34kt.
Armament: 8 SS-N-14 launchers; 2 RBU 6000 and 2 RBU 1000 launchers; 2 twin SA-N-3 launchers; 2 twin 57mm guns; 4 30mm Gatling guns; 2 quintuple 21in (533mm) torpedo tubes.
Aircraft: 1 Ka-25 Hormone-A.
ASW sensors: (Hull-mounted) LF sonar.
Complement: 400.

The Kresta-II class resulted from the crash ASW building programme of the late 1960s and is a modification of the Kresta-I missile cruiser, with ASW weapons systems replacing the anti-ship fit of the earlier vessels. There are two quadruple launcher bins for the SS-N-14 ASW missiles, the first installation on a Soviet ship and one which caused great puzzlement among Western experts who long thought it to be an anti-ship weapon. A significant modification is the construction of a landing platform over the low quarterdeck, the extra height thus gained facilitating take-off and landing of the Kamov Ka-25 Hormone-A ASW helicopter. The two-tier hangar, the roof of which has to be raised to enable the helicopter to be positioned on the lift (which then descends to become the hangar floor at the next deck level), appears complicated but must be successful as it has been followed in later classes of Soviet ships.

A medium-frequency sonar is fitted in the bow position, but it may well be inadequate to exploit fully the 25nm (45km) range of the SS-N-14; thus at longer ranges the ship may have to rely on external data sources, either from its own helicopter or from other ships in the group.

The Kresta-II class continued in production at a rate of one per year until 1976 and is clearly regarded by the Soviet Navy as a successful design, despite the limited number of ASW missiles carried (there are no reloads). Most units serve with the Northern Fleet, and they have frequently operated in company with Kiev class carriers. Other units serve with the Pacific Fleet.

Below: Kresta-II ASW cruiser at anchor in the Mediterranean, with her Ka-25 Hormone-A helicopter leaving on a sortie. This class of ten ships was the result of an urgent programme in the 1960s to produce an ASW version of the Kresta-I, which was optimised for anti-surface ship warfare. The low hangar roof opens to admit the helicopter which is lowered on a lift.

Kanin Class

Destroyers (Soviet Union)

Eight ships

Displacement: 3,700 tons standard; 4,700 tons full load.
Dimensions: Overall length 456ft (139m); beam 48ft (15m); draught 16ft (5m).
Propulsion: Geared steam turbines, 84,000shp; 2 shafts; 34kt.
Armament: 3 MBU 6000 launchers; 1 twin SA-N-1 launcher; 2 quadruple 57mm guns; 4 twin 30mm guns; 10 21in (533mm) torpedo tubes.
Aircraft: None.
ASW sensors: (Hull-mounted) LF sonar.
Complement: 350.

Above: Kanin class in the Caribbean, making excessive smoke.

These eight ships were originally Krupny class missile ships, but when their SS-N-1s became obsolescent in the mid-1960s it was decided to convert them to the ASW role. The conversions were undertaken at the Zhdanov Yard, Leningrad, and later at Komsomolsk during the years 1968 to 1977.

A new medium-frequency sonar was installed in the bow position and three MBU 6000 mortars were fitted, two of them abreast the tower and the third on the forecastle. The existing triple torpedo tube mountings were replaced by the quintuple version, the bridge was enlarged and the electronics were updated. A helicopter platform was fitted aft, but no hangar is provided. All Kanins now have four twin 30mm Gatling mounts abreast the second funnel and Drum Tilt fire-control radars on a newly fitted platform on the rear of the tower.

The Kanin class appears to be a successful conversion and has adequate ASW facilities, although the weapons themselves are somewhat dated by modern standards. Most ships of the class serve with either the Northern or the Pacific Fleet. The absence of a helicopter will, however, be an enduring shortcoming.

Below: Early Kanin, lacking 30mm Gatlings and Bass Tilt radar.

Pauk Class

Fast attack craft—patrol (Soviet Union)

Twelve ships (+)

Displacement: 700 tons full load.
Dimensions: Length overall 187ft (57m); beam 34·4ft (10·5m); draught 6·6ft (2m).
Propulsion: Diesels, 12,000bhp; 2 shafts; 26kt.
Armament: 2 RBU 1200 launchers; 1 3in (76mm) gun; 1 30mm Gatling gun; 1 SA-N-5 launcher; 4 15·7in (400mm) torpedo tubes.
Aircraft: None.
ASW sensors: Dipping sonar on transom.
Complement: 80.

The Soviet Navy's Pauk design is especially interesting as being one of the smallest specialised anti-submarine ships. First seen by Western observers in 1980, Pauk is intended to be the replacement for the ageing Poti class and it would appear that, unusually for them, the Soviets have adopted the hull of the Tarantul class missile ship rather than develop a new one.

The ASW sensor and weapon fit is probably as comprehensive as could possibly be installed in a hull of this size. There is a prominent housing for a dipping sonar on the transom, making the Pauk the smallest ship to carry such a device; there may well also be a hull-mounted sonar in the bow

position, but this is as yet unconfirmed. Main ASW weapons are four single 15·7in (400mm) electric-powered acoustic homing torpedoes, mounted amidships. There are also two RBU 1200 250mm ASW mortars for close-in attack and, for good measure, two six-round depth-charge racks mounted at the stern on either side of the VDS housing.

The Soviet predilection for ever larger guns is followed on the Pauk which has a single 76mm in a dual-purpose mounting on the forecastle and well clear of the superstructure, giving it an excellent field of fire. For close-in air defence there is an ADG6-30 six-barrelled 30mm Gatling on the after superstructure, together with an SA-N-5 Grail SAM launcher below it on the quarterdeck. These air defence weapons systems are controlled by a single Bass Tilt director, mounted on a pedestal at the after end of the bridge structure. The propulsion system is all-diesel, exhaust outlets being located in the hull sides. With an assessed 12,000shp, these should give a maximum speed in the region of 26kt.

As in so many other classes, the Soviet naval architects have managed to pack a great deal into a small hull, and this class represents a substantial addition to the Soviet short-range ASW forces. Western ship designers could well take note of this class, which will undoubtedly be built in large numbers.

Below: Typical of the Soviet ability to pack a lot of weapons into a small hull is this Pauk class FAC. ASW weapons include RBU 1200 launchers and torpedoes. Large stern housing is for VDS.

Krivak-I/II Classes

Frigates (Soviet Union)
Twenty-one/eleven ships

Displacement: 3,000 tons standard; 3,800 tons full load.
Dimensions: Length overall 401·8ft (122·5m); beam 45·9ft (14m); draught 15·4ft (4·7m).
Propulsion: 4 gas turbines, 72,000shp; 2 shafts; 32kt.
Armament: 4 SS-N-14 launchers; 4 SA-N-4 launchers; 2 RBU 6000 launchers; 2 twin 3in (76mm) guns (two singles in Krivak-I); 8 21in (533mm) torpedo tubes.
Aircraft: None.
ASW sensors: (Hull-mounted) LF sonar; (VDS) MF sonar.
Complement: 220.

The Krivak class was first seen by Western observers in 1970 and its long, sleek lines and ingenious combination of armament and effective propulsion system has frequently given rise to admiring comment. Although it followed the Kashin in chronological terms, this is a completely new design, being smaller, easier to build, and possessing an altogether more sophisticated ASW system. Ease of construction has enabled the smaller shipyards on the Baltic and Black Seas to be utilised, leaving the larger yards free for major warships.

The task of the Krivaks is ASW and the most important weapons system is the SS-N-14, which is mounted in a rather inelegant quadruple launcher on the forecastle. This is backed up by two RBU 6000 launchers forward of the bridge and two quadruple torpedo tubes amidships. A bow sonar is fitted and there is a VDS at the stern. The complement of ASW missiles is small by Western standards, but perhaps the most critical deficiency is the lack of an on-board ASW helicopter to provide target data and independent ASW at long ranges; air defence and ECM capability are also not really adequate for open-ocean operations. The ships are, however, clearly adequate for what the Soviet Naval High Command requires, as production has continued for many years, ending only recently with the completion of a total of 21 Krivak-I and 11 Krivak-II, the latter having two single 100mm guns instead of two twin 76mm in the 'X' and 'Y' positions.

One-third of the Krivaks are in the Baltic, where the class is the major ASW unit. The remaining ships serve with the other three fleets, complementing the ASW force provided by their larger compatriots. A successor class is probably about to appear.

Above: Krivak-II frigate in the Mediterranean. The housing and door for the VDS are prominent on the quarterdeck. Although an admired design, the lack of a helicopter is a serious deficiency.

Below: The layout of the Krivak-I is clearly seen in this view. ASW weapons are the SS-N-14 launcher on the foredeck, two RBU 6000 before the bridge and two quad torpedo tubes amidships.

Dédalo Class

ASW carrier (Spain)

One ship

Displacement: 13,000 tons standard; 16,416 tons full load.
Dimensions: Length overall 623ft (189·9m); beam 109·1ft (33·3m); draught 26ft (7·9m).
Propulsion: Geared steam turbines, 100,000shp; 4 shafts; 24kt.
Armament: 26 40mm guns.
Aircraft: 5 AV-8S Matador; 8 SH-3D Sea King; 4 AB 212ASW.
ASW sensors: None.
Complement: 1,112 (inc. air group).

To provide themselves with a 'quick-fix' air component in the 1960s the Spanish Navy leased from the US Navy a World War II light carrier (itself a converted cruiser hull). Used as an ASW carrier, *Dédalo* was purchased outright in 1973, and in 1976 Spain acquired a number of AV-8S Harriers (Matadors) from the USA to provide a limited attack capability. *Dédalo* is currently the flagship of the Spanish fleet but will be replaced by the *Príncipe de Asturias* (qv) in 1985–86. The whole *Dédalo* project is a good example of what can be achieved at small cost and using only limited resources if ambitions are curbed and operational requirements kept within reasonable limits.

Below: First built as a Cleveland class cruiser for the US Navy in 1942 and then converted to an aircraft transport, this ship was reactivated in 1967, fitted out as a helicopter carrier and leased to the Royal Spanish Navy. Six years later she was bought outright and has since served as the flagship of the fleet.

Príncipe de Asturias Class

ASW carrier (Spain)
One ship

Displacement: 14,700 tons full load.
Dimensions: Length overall 640ft (195·1m); beam 81ft (24·7m); draught 29·8ft (9·1m).
Propulsion: COGAG; 2 LM2500 gas turbines, 46,600shp; 1 shaft; 26kt.
Armament: 4 Meroka CIWS.
Aircraft: 17 mixed V/STOL and helicopters.
ASW sensors: None.
Complement: 793 (inc. air group).

Príncipe de Asturias has been built to replace *Dédalo* (qv). The design is based on that of the ill-fated US Navy Sea Control Ship of the early 1970s to provide ASW and air superiority missions in low-threat areas. A simple design with single-shaft propulsion and an austere electronic fit, *Príncipe de Asturias* is built around her aviation facilities, which include a full-width hangar occupying the after two-thirds of the ship. A feature not in the original SCS design is the full 12° ski-jump which will enable the AV-8S Matadors to take off with maximum payload. The only fixed armament is four Spanish-designed Meroka 20mm close-in weapons systems. *Príncipe de Asturias* was laid down in 1979 and launched on 22 May 1982.

The air wing will comprise 6–8 AV-8S Matadors, 6–8 SH-3 Sea Kings for the ASW role, and 4–8 troop-carrying helicopters. As with *Dédalo*, the Spanish Navy has shown what can be done on a limited budget if sufficient thought and sound judgement is applied. The new ship may be unsophisticated by the standards of the larger navies, but the fact is that she will give the Spanish Navy a seaborne air capability which it would otherwise lack.

Below: Based on the US Navy's Sea Control Ship concept *Príncipe de Asturias* will operate both helicopters and V/STOL aircraft.

Invincible Class

Light aircraft carriers (UK)
Three ships

Displacement: 16,256 tons standard; 19,812 tons full load.
Dimensions: Length overall 677ft (206·3m); beam 105ft (32m); draught 24ft (7·3m).
Propulsion: COGAG; 4 Rolls-Royce Olympus TM3B gas turbines, 112,000shp; 2 shafts; 28kt.
Armament: 1 twin Sea Dart launcher (22 missiles); 2 Phalanx CIWS.
Aircraft: 5 Sea Harrier FRS.1; 9 Sea King HAS.5; 2 Sea King AEW.
ASW sensors: (Hull-mounted) Type 2016.
Complement: 1,000 (+320 air group).

It is indisputable that without the air cover provided by HMS *Invincible* and the older *Hermes* the British task force could never have succeeded in re-establishing British rule over the Falkland Islands in the South Atlantic war of 1982. In fact, the British were very lucky to have these carriers at all, especially the *Invincible*, which has had a very checkered history and was very nearly cancelled on several occasions. Initially this class was to operate large ASW helicopters, but late in the design process provision was made for operating Sea Harrier aircraft to intercept hostile reconnaissance and

Below: HMS *Illustrious* (R06) at sea. The three ships of this class serve as flagships of ASW groups, and the air group includes Sea King ASW helicopters and Sea Harrier V/STOL aircraft.

ASW patrol aircraft. A final change in 1976–77 required the ships to be able to act as commando carriers as well!

The hangar has a 'dumb-bell' shape, with a narrow centre-section and wide bays at each end, dictated by the large exhaust uptakes for the gas turbines to starboard and imposing some constraints on the movement of fixed-wing aircraft within it. Unlike earlier RN carriers, the Invincible class has an open forecastle. The 600ft (182·9m) x 44ft (13·4m) flight deck is offset to port and angled slightly to avoid the Sea Dart launcher which is fairly central on the foredeck. *Invincible* and *Illustrious* have a 7° ski-jump at the forward end of the flight deck, which enables the Sea Harrier to increase its payload by some 1,500lb (680kg). *Ark Royal,* however, will have a 12° ski-jump, which means that the Sea Dart launcher will have to be moved. Following experience in the Falkland Islands, US Vulcan/Phalanx close-in defence weapons have been installed, one beside the Sea Dart launcher forward and the second on the after end of the flight deck.

A further lesson from the Falklands has led to the inclusion of two Sea King AEW helicopters in the air wing. During that conflict *Invincible* operated between eight and twelve Sea Harrier/Harrier GR.3 aircraft in addition to her complement of Mk 5 Sea Kings. Her sistership *Illustrious*, which relieved her in the summer of 1982, operated ten Sea Harriers while on patrol in the South Atlantic. The limited hangar capacity means that a permanent deck park must be operated.

For the NATO EASTLANT role, which remains their primary mission, the Invincibles are equipped with a sophisticated ASW command centre and first-rate communications. They are also fitted with Type 184 hull sonar but have no shipborne ASW weapons. The planned sale of *Invincible* to Australia has been cancelled.

Broadsword Class

Destroyers (UK)

Six ships + 2 building + 4 ordered

Displacement: 3,500 tons standard; 4,000 tons full load.
Dimensions: Length overall 430ft (131·2m); beam 48·5ft (14·8m); draught 14ft (4·3m).
Propulsion: 2 Rolls-Royce Olympus gas turbines, 56,000shp; 2 Rolls-Royce Tyne gas turbines, 8500shp; 2 shafts; 30+kt.
Armament: 4 Exocet SSM launchers; 2 6-barrelled Seawolf SAM launchers; 2 40mm guns; 2 triple Mk 32 torpedo tubes.
Aircraft: 2 WG13 Lynx.
ASW sensors: Type 2016; Type 2008.
Complement: 223.

The *Broadsword* class is the successor to the very successful Leander class (qv), the first of these new ships being ordered on 8 February 1974, launched in May 1976 and commissioned on 3 May 1979. The remaining seven of the class are following at approximately yearly intervals. This class is designed primarily for ASW and has a comprehensive weapons and sensor fit for the role. The ships are also fitted out as group leaders and are fully capable of acting as 'Officer in Tactical Command' (OTC) command ships.

Above: HMS *Battleaxe* (F89), second of the Royal Navy's Type 22 destroyers; later ships of the class are 41ft (12·5m) longer.

Right: HMS *Broadsword* (F88) with Lynx ASW helicopter. Note the triple torpedo tubes abaft the ship's boat.

The main ASW sensor is the Type 2016 sonar, the roll-stabilised array being mounted in a GRP keel dome in line with RN practice. ASW weapons are two triple Mk 32 torpedo tubes firing Mk 46 torpedoes. Batch I and II ships (the first four of the class) have only two 40mm guns and their main armament is all-missile, the first RN warship class to attempt this transition. However, the Falklands War proved that this was an error, and Batch III ships will have a single 4·5in (115mm) DP gun. The ships also have a hangar and flight deck for two WG13 Lynx ASW helicopters, although only one is normally carried in peacetime.

The Batch III ships are being constructed 41ft (12·5m) longer than the earlier ships, bringing overall length up to 471ft (143·6m). The first two are reported to cost an estimated £120 million each (1981 prices), a fearsome price and one which is indicative of the rapidly escalating costs of modern defence equipment.

These ships are amongst the most sophisticated ASW vessels afloat and have already established a good reputation for efficiency and effectiveness. *Broadsword* and *Brilliant* of the class took part in the South Atlantic War in 1982, where their Seawolf missiles proved of great value.

Leander Class

Frigates (UK)

Forty-four ships

Displacement: (Batch 3) 2,500 tons standard; 2,962 tons full load.
Dimensions: (Batch 3) length overall 372ft (113·4m); beam 43ft (13·1m); draught 18ft (5·5m).
Propulsion: 2 geared turbines, 30,000shp; 2 shafts; 28kt.
Armament: Depends upon group. 'Ikara' group has two quadruple Seacat SAM launchers, 2 40mm guns and Ikara ASW system; 'Exocet' group has 4 Exocet launchers, 3 quadruple Seacat launchers, 2 40mm guns, and 2 triple torpedo tubes; 'broad-beamed' group has 1 twin 4·5in (114mm) gun, 2 20mm guns and Limbo mortar.
Aircraft: 1 Wasp (WG13 Lynx in *Phoebe* and *Sirius*).
ASW sensors: (Hull-mounted) Type 170, Type 184 (Batch 1); Type 184 (Batch 2); Type 2016 (Batch 3).
Complement: 257 (Batch 1); 223 (Batch 2); 260 (Batch 3).

The first unit of the very successful Leander class was laid down on 10 April 1959 and commissioned on 27 March 1963. The class was the first RN design to include a helicopter and represents the largest single group of ship to be built for the Royal Navy for many years: twenty-six serve with the Royal Navy and others of the class serve with the navies of Australia(2), Chile (2), India (6), the Netherlands (6) and New Zealand (2). The ships were designed specifically for ASW duties and carried a hull-mounted sonar, stern-mounted VDS (since removed) and a variety of ASW weapons. The last ten of the class were 2ft (0·6m) broader to improve stability, and have become known, somewhat inelegantly, as the 'broad-beamed Leanders'.

A whole series of conversions has taken place, some of them not yet completed. These involve fitting either the Ikara ASW system or Exocet SSMs, both at the expense of the twin 4·5in (114mm) gun mounting, a step which will doubtless be regretted following the South Atlantic War. It is an astonishing comment on modern costs that HMS *Argonaut*, which cost £7 million to build, was converted to an Exocet type in 1977–80 at a cost of £62·6 million!

Right: HMS *Aurora* (F10) following her Ikara refit. Forty-four of this very successful class have been built for six navies. Developed from the Type 12 they are intended specifically for ASW duties. In the RN three types now exist: one armed with Ikara, one with Exocet, and the third, the 'broad-beamed Leanders', have Exocet and Sea Wolf SAMs. They will serve into the 1990s.

Amazon Class

Frigates (UK)

Six ships

Displacement: 2,750 tons standard; 3,250 tons full load.
Dimensions: Length overall 384ft (117m); beam 40·5ft (12·3m); draught 19ft (5·8m).
Propulsion: 2 Rolls-Royce Olympus gas turbines, 56,000shp; 2 Rolls-Royce Tyne gas turbines, 8,500shp; 2 shafts; 30kt.
Armament: 4 Exocet SSM launchers; 1 4·5in (114mm) gun; 1 quadruple Seacat launcher; 2 20mm guns; 2 triple torpedo tubes.
Aircraft: 1 WG13 Lynx.
ASW sensors: (Hull-mounted) Type 184M.
Complement: 175.

Before the first of the 'broad-beamed' Leander class frigates had been laid down, Vosper-Thornycroft received a contract for a new design to be prepared in collaboration with Yarrow. They produced the Type 21 Amazon class, the first being launched in 1971 and commissioned in 1974. They were the first Royal Navy ships to be designed from the outset to be powered solely by gas turbines, and were also the first for many years to be designed by a commercial firm.

The ASW fit includes a Type 184M hull-mounted sonar, and the ASW armament comprises two triple torpedo tubes for Mk 48 torpedoes; the ships also have a flight deck and hangar for the Westland WG13 Lynx ASW helicopter. Other armament includes a 4·5in (114mm) main gun in a DP mounting, four Exocet SSMs, a Seacat SAM launcher and two 20mm Oerlikon cannon. Despite this heavy armament (relative to the hull size), the complement is only 175 officers and ratings.

Each of the Amazons has some 135 tons of aluminium alloy in its structure and the spectacular destruction of *Amazon* and *Antelope* during the South Atlantic War led to reports that it was the aluminium that was responsible. This was investigated fully after the war and the chairman of the working party stated that he was 'not aware of any evidence to suggest that any ship was lost because of the use of aluminium alloys in its construction. Nor was there any evidence that aluminium or aluminium alloys had burned' (*Financial Times*, 24 December 1982).

These are handsome ships that have served the Royal Navy well, and it is indeed sad that two out of the eight should have been lost in a war. It is also worth noting that no fewer than seven out of the eight in the class were in the Falklands area during the war.

Below: HMS *Ambuscade* (F172). This after quarter picture clearly shows the flight deck and hangar for the Lynx ASW helicopter.

Spruance/Kidd Classes

Destroyers (USA)

Thirty-four (+1 building)/four ships

Displacement: 5,830 tons light; 7,810 tons full load.
Dimensions: Length overall 563·2ft (171·7m); beam 55·1ft (16·8m); draught 19ft (5·8m).
Propulsion: 4 LM2500 gas turbines, 80,000shp; 2 shafts; 33kt.
Armament: 2 quadruple Harpoon SSM launchers; 1 octuple Sea Sparrow SAM launcher; 2 single 5in (127mm) guns; 2 Phalanx CIWS; 1 ASROC launcher; 2 triple Mk 32 torpedo tubes. See text.
Aircraft: 1 SH-3 Sea King or 2 SH-2D.
ASW sensors: (Hull-mounted) SQS-53.
Complement: 296.
(Specifications given for Spruance class; see text for Kidd class variations.)

The Spruance class was designed to replace war-built destroyers of the Gearing and Sumner classes. At 7,800 tons full load (twice the displacement of the ships it has replaced) the Spruance epitomises the philosophy which envisages the construction of large hulls with block superstructures (maximising internal volume) fitted with easily maintained machinery and equipped with high-technology sensors and weapons that can be added to or updated by modular replacement at a later stage. The aim is to minimise 'platform' costs and maximise expenditure on weapons systems ('payload').

Above: USS *Chandler* (DDG-996), one of the four-ship Kidd class.

The advanced ASW features of the Spruances are largely hidden. The ASROC launcher, for example, has a magazine containing no fewer than 24 reloads. The large hangar to port of the after funnel accommodates two LAMPS III helicopters, while the triple Mk 32 torpedo tubes are concealed behind sliding doors. The bow sonar is the SQS-53, which can operate in a variety of active and passive modes, including direct path, bottom-bounce and convergence zone. This has proved so successful that the SQS-35 VDS originally scheduled for the class will not now be fitted.

The adoption of an all-gas-turbine propulsion system, which employs paired LM2500 turbines en échelon, is an arrangement which not only gives easy maintenance and reduces manning but also significantly cuts underwater noise emission. The class is fitted with computerised data-handling systems in a well-designed Combat Information Centre (CIC), and also has the Mk 86 Gunfire Control System (GFCS) and the Mk 116 Underwater Fire Control System (UFCS).

The flexibility of the Spruance design is such that it formed the basis for the new Ticonderoga class Aegis cruisers, and for the four ships ordered for the Imperial Iranian Navy (but acquired for the USN in 1979 following the fall of the Shah and now designated the Kidd class). These were completed for the Iranians for the AAW role, having, for example, twin-arm Mk 26 launchers in place of the original ASROC and Sea Sparrow launchers. However, the ASROC missiles can still be fired from the forward Mk 26 launcher, and the SQS-53 sonar is fitted. Thus the Kidds have an ASW capability not too far short of the Spruances and the gap will doubtless be narrowed in the course of future refits.

One additional ship of the Spruance class was ordered in 1979. This ship (DD997) was to have had increased hangar and flight-deck space to operate both helicopters and VTOL aircraft, but it will now be completed as a standard vessel. The US Navy also plans to build more Spruances (starting in FY86) to replace the fourteen destroyers of the Sherman and Hull ▶ classes (qv).

Left: USS *Elliott* (DDG-967), a Spruance class ASW destroyer. 35 of this class have been ordered, which, with the ships of the Kidd class, represent a major addition to the US Navy.

► Following a great deal of controversy, the Spruance and Kidd classes are now firmly established as one of the most successful and capable of modern destroyer designs, with an outstanding ASW performance. Thirty-four are now in service, one is building, and there is the probability of at least ten more. Altogether they make a major contribution to countering the Soviet underwater threat, and will continue to do so well into the next century.

Below: USS *Briscoe* (DDG-977). The apparently sparse armament of these ships has led ill-informed critics to disparage the design. In fact, the Spruances are excellent ASW ships and are not only well-armed, but also have numerous reloads in the capacious hulls for all systems, something lacking in Soviet designs. For example, there are 24 reloads for the ASROC launcher seen on the forecastle, and 500 rounds for the 5in (127mm) gun.

Forrest Sherman/Decatur Classes

Destroyers (USA)

Fourteen/four ships

Displacement: 3,000 tons standard; 4,200 tons full load.
Dimensions: Length overall 418ft (127·4m); beam 45ft (13·7m); draught 23ft (7m).
Propulsion: 2 geared turbines, 70,000shp; 2 shafts; 33kt.
Armament: 2 5in (127mm) guns; 1 ASROC launcher; 2 triple Mk 32 torpedo tubes.
Aircraft: None.
ASW sensors: (Hull-mounted) SQS-23; (VDS) SQS-35. See text.
Complement: 324.
(Specifications given for ASW Forrest Sherman class; see text for Decatur class variations.)

The first postwar US destroyers, the Forrest Sherman class, were conventionally armed but followed the (then) current tactical thinking in abandoning anti-ship torpedoes, which were replaced by four fixed 21in (533mm) 'long' ASW torpedoes and in mounting fewer guns with a higher performance than their war-built predecessors. The conventional armament was quickly overtaken by new technological developments—especially the nuclear-powered submarine and the surface-to-air missile—and an extensive conversion programme was drawn up in the early 1960s.

Eight ships were given a limited ASW conversion between 1967 and 1971. In this the second gun mounting was replaced by an ASROC launcher and the fixed ASW tubes by triple, trainable Mk 32 tubes, whilst surveillance radars were updated and a VDS was fitted at the stern. Even this limited conversion programme ran into cost problems and the remaining six ships of the class received only those modifications which entailed the minimum of structural alteration. They retained all three 5in (127mm) guns and were not fitted with ASROC or VDS.

Four ships of the class underwent a major conversion in the years 1965–68 and are now known as the separate Decatur class. The three-year

Above: USS *Turner Joy* (DD-951) of the Forrest Sherman class. The first class of destroyers to be built for the US Navy after World War II, they have undergone major conversions to keep pace with the advances in performance of Soviet submarines.

Left: USS *John Paul Jones* (DDG-32) of the Decatur class, four ships which started life as part of the Forrest Sherman class.

refit included the replacement of the after 5in (127mm) guns by the Tartar missile system. A Mk 13 single-arm launcher, together with its cylindrical magazine, replaced the after turret, and immediately forward of it a large deckhouse carrying a single SPG-51 tracker/illuminator was constructed. Two massive lattice masts give the ships a distinctive profile, carrying the large SPS-48 3-D radar antenna. The initial conversion plans envisaged the operation of DASH ASW drones, but when the DASH programme ran into difficulties an ASROC launcher was fitted instead.

The ASW capabilities of this class are now somewhat dated, and a serious limitation is the lack of an on-board helicopter. All these ships are due to be replaced by new-build Spruance class DDs in the early 1990s.

Oliver Hazard Perry Class

Frigates (USA)

Forty-seven ships + 5 building + 15 ordered

Displacement: 3,605 tons full load.
Dimensions: Length overall 445ft (135·6m); beam 45ft (13·7m); draught 14·8ft (4·5m).
Propulsion: 2 gas turbines, 41,000shp; 1 shaft; 29kt.
Armament: 1 Mk 13 Harpoon/Standard launcher; 1 3in (76mm) gun; 1 Phalanx CIWS; 2 triple Mk 32 torpedo tubes.
Aircraft: 2 SH-2.
ASW sensors: (Hull-mounted) SQS-56.
Complement: 210.

The Oliver Hazard Perry (FFG7) class originated in the 'Patrol Frigate' programme which was to constitute the 'low' end of a high/low mix, providing large numbers of cheap escorts with reduced capabilities. These were to balance the sophisticated and very costly specialist ASW and AAW ships whose primary mission was to protect carriers. Strict limitations were placed on cost, displacement and manpower, and the FFG7 was to be built in small yards, keeping construction techniques simple, making the maximum use of flat panels and bulkheads, and ensuring that passageways kept deliberately straight. The hull structure is prefabricated in modules of 35, 100, 200 or 400 tons, allowing the shipyards to select the most convenient size.

Like the previous frigate classes, the Perry has only one screw, but the layout is much more compact as the result of using gas turbines. Two LM2500s (the same model as in the Spruances) are located side by side in a single engine room, and small retractable propulsion pods are fitted just aft of the sonar dome to provide emergency 'get-you-home' power as well as help docking. Each of these pods has a 325hp engine, and the two together can propel the ship at a speed of some 10kt.

Above: USS *Oliver Hazard Perry* (FFG-7), nameship of a class of 67 frigates. Their design makes them appear small but they are, in fact, larger than the British Leanders. Cost escalation has resulted in a FY80 unit price of $200·6 million.

Left: Three Perry class frigates en echelon: USS *Jack Williams* (FFG-24) in the lead, with USS *Antrim* (FFG-20) and *Oliver Hazard Perry* (FFG-7).

The armament is oriented more towards AAW than that of the Knox, which was a specialist ASW design. The FFG7 has a Mk 13 launcher forward for Standard (MR) SAMs and Harpoon ASMs and an OTO Melara 3in (76mm) gun on top of the superstructure. ASROC is not fitted, but there is a large hangar aft for two LAMPS helicopters. The SQS-56 sonar is hull-mounted inside a rubber dome; it is a new austere type, much less sophisticated than the SQS-26. It was planned, however, that the FFG7 would operate in company with other frigates equipped with the SQS-26 and would receive target information from their sensors via data links.

The FFG7 has been tailored to accommodate only those systems envisaged in the near future, including the SH-60 LAMPS III, the SQR-19 towed tactical array, fin stabilisers, the Link 11 data transfer system and a single Phalanx CIWS. Once these have been installed, however, there remains only a further 50-ton margin for additional equipment.

Forty of the class are currently in service, with a further five building and another 15 on order. Four have been built in the USA for the Royal Australian Navy, and three are being built by Bazan at Ferrol for the Spanish Navy.

Knox Class

Frigates (USA)

Fifty-one ships

Displacement: 3,011 tons standard; 3,877 tons full load.
Dimensions: Length overall 438ft (133·5m); beam 46·8ft (14·3m); draught 15ft (4·6m).
Propulsion: 1 geared turbine, 35,000shp; 1 shaft; 27kt.
Armament: 1 octuple Harpoon launcher; 1 5in (127mm) gun; 1 ASROC launcher; 4 fixed Mk 32 torpedo tubes. See text.
Aircraft: 1 SH-2.
ASW sensors: (Hull-mounted) SQS-26; (VDS) SQS-35. See text.
Complement: 245.

The Knox class began as a design for a missile escort, but Congressional opposition led to it being redesigned as an ASW escort. Although it retains the one-shaft propulsion system of the Garcia/Brooke design, the complicated pressure-fired boilers of the latter were abandoned in favour of a safer, more conventional steam plant. This resulted in an increase in size without creating any extra space for weapons or sensors.

Above: USS *Stein* (FF-1065) a frigate of the 51-strong Knox class.

After many changes in the early stages, the armament now provides a first-class ASW outfit. There is a reloadable ASROC launcher before the bridge and a hull-mounted SQS-26 sonar. Aft is a hangar with a telescopic extension and a fair-sized flight deck for a LAMPS I ASW helicopter.

Besides the Sea Sparrow BPDMS, all but eleven ships have received the SQS-35 VDS since completion; all except the same eleven will receive the SQR-18A TACTASS towed sonar array in the near future. Most ships have had their ASROC launchers modified to fire Harpoon, and it is planned to replace the Sea Sparrow missile system with a single Phalanx CIWS.

In spite of some early problems the Knox has become one of the most useful and versatile classes of US warship. It also forms the largest class of major combatants built in the West since the war: 46 have been built for the US Navy and a further five in Spain.

Left: USS *Roark* (FF-1053), here seen at sea in the Pacific, was the second ship of the class. Designed to operate the DASH ASW helicopter drone, they have all been modified to take the LAMPS II (Kaman SH-2D) helicopter, a great improvement.

Below: USS *Harold E Holt* (FF-1074) achieved fame when she played a crucial role in the rescue of the crew of the *Mayaguez* in 1976.

Brooke Class

Frigates (USA)

Six ships

Displacement: 2,640 tons standard; 3,426 tons full load.
Dimensions: Length overall 414·5ft (126·3m); beam 44·2ft (13·5m); draught 15ft (4·6m).
Propulsion: 1 geared turbine, 35,000shp; 1 shaft; 27kt.
Armament: 1 Mk 22 Tartar/Standard launcher; 1 5in (127mm) gun; 1 ASROC launcher; 2 triple Mk 32 torpedo tubes.
Aircraft: 1 SH-2D.
ASW sensors: (Hull-mounted) SQS-26AX.
Complement: 248.

The Brooke and Garcia classes share the same hull, single-shaft propulsion plant and general layout, but the Brookes have a single Mk 22 Tartar launcher in place of the second 5in (127mm) Mk 30 gun of the Garcias. This Mk 22 launcher has a single-ring magazine with a capacity of 16 rounds, and the above-water sensor outfit is also comparatively austere. Despite this, Congress baulked at the $11 million increase in cost over the gun-armed Garcia design, and stopped construction after six units had been built.

Since completion the Brookes have undergone similar modifications to the Garcias: the stern Mk 25 torpedo tubes have been removed and, following the abandonment of the DASH programme, the hangar has been enlarged to accommodate a LAMPS helicopter. All ships of the class have a bow-mounted SQS-26AX sonar.

Below: USS *Richard L Page* (FFG-5) in Narragansett Bay. The Brooke class are basically similar to the Garcias, but have a Tartar missile system in place of the after 5in gun. The last three Brookes to be built have an automatic loading system for the ASROC anti-submarine missile launcher mounted on the forecastle (seen here behind the 5in gun turret).

Garcia Class

Frigates (USA)

Ten ships

Displacement: 2,620 tons standard; 3,403 tons full load.
Dimensions: Length overall 414·5ft (126·3m); beam 44·2ft (13·5m); draught 15ft (4·6m).
Propulsion: 1 geared turbine, 35,000shp; 1 shaft; 27·5kt.
Armament: 2 single 5in (127mm) guns; 1 ASROC launcher; 2 triple Mk 32 torpedo tubes.
Aircraft: 1 SH-2D. See text.
ASW sensors: (Hull-mounted) SQS-26AXR.
Complement: 247 (first four ships 239).

The Garcia class ocean escort was evolved from the Bronstein design which, although similar in size to contemporary European escorts, has proved too small for the US Navy. Improvements included a larger, flush-decked hull, a heavier gun armament and provision aft for DASH drones (an ASW programme since abandoned). The last five ships were also given a reload magazine for ASROC at the forward end of the bridge, which thus has a distinctive sloping face. All except *Sample* and *Albert David* (which are fitted instead with a towed array) had their hangars enlarged and a telescopic extension fitted to enable them to operate manned LAMPS helicopters, giving a significant increase in ASW capability.

A compact, one-shaft steam propulsion plant employing pressure-fired boilers was adopted in order to maximise the internal volume available for weapons and electronics. This proved complex to operate and maintain, and concern about the reliability of such a high-technology system, especially in a ship with only a single shaft, led to a reversion to conventional boilers in the succeeding Knox class.

Below: USS *Bradley* (FF-1041). The telescopic hangar is partially extended; originally designed to take the abortive DASH drone these ships had to be modified to take the LAMPS SH-2D helicopter.

Nuclear-Powered Attack Submarines (SSN)

Some twenty years ago it was being confidently pre-
dicted that nuclear-powered submarines would take
over from conventionally-powered vessels in all but the
smallest navies. This has not happened, mainly because
of the expense and resources (especially technical
manpower) required for the SSNs, and, as shown later
in the book, there are still many hundreds of SSKs in
service. Nevertheless, the numbers of SSNs and SSN-
users are growing year by year, with France and the
People's Republic of China the latest to add such boats
to their fleets.

The SSN combines in its hull considerable carrying
capacity with endurance. The carrying capacity is
devoted to weapons and sensors, while the endurance
frees the submarines from that most vulnerable of all
activities, approaching the surface—except when the
need arises to communicate with base.

The key element in an SSN's sensors is the sonar, and
in their submarines US designers have devised large
'conformal' sonar arrays which take up the entire bow.
This has meant that the torpedo tubes have had to be
moved further back on the hull and are now angled
outwards at some 10°, although this approach has not
been followed by other SSN-equipped navies. One of
the problems facing SSNs is that their sensors out-
perform their weapons, especially the torpedo, which
is a relatively slow-travelling device and reasonably
easy to detect. Thus both the Soviet and US Navies
have introduced submarine-launched missiles which
travel for most of their journey through the air, delivering their payload in the vicinity of the target and
ideally giving him insufficient time for evasive action.

The Soviet Alfa class is a very significant design:
made of titanium, and coated with anechoic tiles, the
boats can travel at over 40kt, posing a major problem to
surface ASW forces (which cannot move at anything
like that speed) and outperforming virtually every
torpedo in service. The US Los Angeles class is not
as fast as the Alfa but represents probably the most
sophisticated warship system ever to enter service.
The French Navy's Rubis design is of interest in that it is
considerably smaller than any other SSN, and the
French are claiming that they have found different
answers to the problems of size and noise in submarine
nuclear propulsion systems from those employed by
the Americans, although no details of the system have
yet been made public. On the other side of the globe
the PLA-Navy now has three Han class SSNs in service.

Above: USS *Bremerton,* a Los Angeles class SSN of the US Navy, running at high speed during her sea trials. The Los Angeles class is certainly the most effective of all SSNs, but the unit price had risen to $495·8 million in FY81, a rate of expenditure which even the US Navy cannot sustain for long. The British, French, Chinese and Soviet Navies also operate SSNs.

Rubis Class (SNA72)

SSN (France)

One boat + 4 building

Displacement: 2,385 tons surfaced; 2,670 tons submerged.
Dimensions: Length 236·5ft (72·1m); beam 24·9ft (7·6m); draught 21ft (6·4m).
Propulsion: Nuclear, 48MW; 1 shaft; 25kt dived.
Armament: Tube-launched SM.39 missiles; 4 21in (533mm) torpedo tubes.
Complement: 66.

France came late on to the nuclear submarine scene and, under strong pressure from President de Gaulle, went straight to SSBNs. Such a massive programme, which for political reasons had to be entirely French in character, took up all the available national resources for many years. It was not until the 1974 naval programme, therefore, that the French Navy was able to turn its attention to SSNs, with the first of the SNA72 class—*Rubis*—being laid down in December 1976 and launched on 7 July 1979. She joined the fleet in 1982, following extensive trials. She will be joined by four more boats in the years 1984–88, and the French intend to form two squadrons, one based at Brest and the other at Toulon.

The SNA72 class are the smallest SSNs in any navy and are based fairly closely on the Agosta class conventional submarines (qv). Such small size suggests that the French have produced a dramatic development in nuclear reactor design, especially compared with the rather large devices in the Le Redoutable class SSBNs.

Armament, sensors and fire control systems are based on those currently in service in the Agostas. Four 21in (533mm) torpedo tubes are fitted, with ten reloads. From 1985 onwards the SNA72 class will be fitted for the SM.39, an adaptation of the very successful MM.38 Exocet surface-launched anti-ship missile; like the US Harpoon, SM.39 will be tube-launched from underwater. A follow-on class of SSNs is already on the drawing boards.

Right: *Rubis* **(S601) first of the class of French nuclear-powered attack sub-marines. Five are currently planned, to form two squadrons: one in the Atlantic, the second in the Mediterranean.**

Below: The second of the SNA72 class, *Saphir* (S602) is launched at Cherbourg (1 September 1981). The size of the hull should be compared with that of the Los Angeles class (qv).

Alfa Class

SSN (Soviet Union)

Twelve boats + 8 building

Displacement: 3,500 tons surfaced; 3,800 tons submerged.
Dimensions: Length 260·1ft (79·3m); beam 32·8ft (10m); draught 24·9ft (7·6m).
Propulsion: Nuclear, 40,000shp; 1 shaft; 40+kt dived.
Armament: 6 21in (533mm) torpedo tubes.
Complement: 60.

The first Alfa class SSN was completed at the Sudomekh Yard in Leningrad in 1970 and after protracted tests was scrapped in 1974, reportedly as a result of a major leak from the nuclear reactor. The second boat was laid down in 1971, the third in 1976 and the fourth in 1977, and production continues at a rate of two per year, with fourteen expected to be in service by 1985. An eventual total of twenty is anticipated.

The Alfa class submarines are much shorter than previous Soviet SSNs, indicating the possibility of a new and much smaller nuclear reactor; some sources suggest that it may be liquid-metal cooled. These boats are very fast and are reported to have run under NATO task forces on exercise at such speeds (40kt) that effective counter-action in a combat environment would have been virtually impossible. The hull is constructed of titanium alloy, this conferring a maximum diving depth of some 3,000ft (914m); indeed, the long construction times may be related to difficulties in fabricating such materials. The long, low fin and the total absence of any protruding devices in any published photographs suggest that great attention has been paid to reducing the noise signature. The hull is coated with Clusterguard, an anechoic substance also designed to resist detection.

There is a large low-frequency sonar array in the bow, and the submarine is fitted with six torpedo tubes and twelve reloads. This class is clearly at the very forefront of submarine technology, and is regarded with great respect by NATO forces. A major concern is that the Alfa's apparent top speed is equal to, or possibly even greater than, the speed of NATO torpedoes, which leaves ASW commanders with a crucial problem.

Below: Alfas are made of titanium and coated with Clusterguard.

Echo-I Class

SSN (Soviet Union)
Five boats

Displacement: 4,300 tons surfaced; 5,200 tons submerged.
Dimensions: Length 373·9ft (114m); beam 29·8ft (9·1m); draught 23·9ft (7·3m).
Propulsion: Nuclear, 30,000shp; 2 shafts; 28kt dived.
Armament: 6 21in (533mm) bow, 2 16in (406mm) stern torpedo tubes.
Complement: 100.

The formidable Echo class SSGNs have for many years been an important part of the Soviet Navy's offensive firepower at sea. Their hulls are generally similar to those of the November class, and they are probably powered by the same nuclear plant, which was the first to be developed in the USSR. Only five Echo-I boats were built, being followed by the longer, more heavily armed Echo-II. Not wishing to waste some perfectly adequate hulls, the Soviet Navy then converted the five Echo-Is from SSGNs to SSNs by removing the missile system and covering over the noisy wells in the casing.

All five Echo-I SSNs serve with the Soviet Pacific Fleet, and one came to grief in a spectacular fashion in August 1980 near Okinawa. It had to be towed back to port and there was a considerble international row when the route chosen took it very close to the Japanese mainland on its way back to the Soviet Union.

Above: Echo-I SSN: five have been converted from SSGNs.

Below: Soviet Echo-I SSN running on the surface. Derived from SSGNs in order not to waste hulls, these boats, like most such conversions, are not particularly effective ASW platforms, being both noisy and slow. They have also been somewhat accident prone, several having limped home in a blaze of publicity.

November Class

SSN (Soviet Union)

Thirteen boats

Displacement: 4,300 tons surfaced; 5,000 tons submerged.
Dimensions: Length 359·8ft (109·7m); beam 29·8ft (9·1m); draught 21·9ft (6·7m).
Propulsion: Nuclear, 30,000shp; 2 shafts; 30kt dived.
Armament: 8 21in (533mm) bow, 2 16in (406mm) stern torpedo tubes.
Complement: 86.

Below: November class SSN displaying the noise-generating free-flood holes and small protrusions on her hull. First nuclear-powered submarines in the Soviet Navy, the November design features a very old-fashioned hull. Thirteen are in service.

These large and conservatively designed boats were the first Soviet submarines to have nuclear propulsion; they entered service in the years 1958–63. The technology was based, to a major extent, upon intelligence information gained from the United States in 1955, though at the time the Soviets seem to have failed to appreciate the advantages of the 'teardrop' hull first seen on the US Navy's Albacore. Accordingly, the Soviet designers gave the Novembers a long, conventionally shaped hull with twin propellers, which, coupled with the many free-flood holes, makes them very noisy boats. By 1963 a total of fifteen had been commissioned, despite the fact that they had long since been overtaken by technology.

One November class submarine sank in the Atlantic south-west of the UK in April 1970. The boat took some time to founder and most, if not all, the crew were saved by Comecon merchant ships which had been rushed to the scene on orders from Moscow. There appeared to have been a total loss of power, although this would not necessarily explain why she foundered. No nuclear contamination has ever been found in the area.

Yankee-III Class

SSN (Soviet Union)

Nine boats

Displacement: 4,600 tons surfaced; 5,600 tons submerged.
Dimensions: Length 329·6ft (100·5m); beam 38ft (11·6m); draught 25ft (7·6m).
Propulsion: Nuclear 40,000shp; 2 shafts; 30kt dived.
Armament: 6 21in (533mm) torpedo tubes.
Complement: 90.

Above: Yankee-I class SSBN. In order to comply with the SALT-I ceilings, nine such Yankees have been withdrawn from service and have had their missile compartment (the raised section abaft the fin) removed. They have then been returned to the fleet as SSNs; a sensible economy measure.

The Yankee class was the first Soviet purpose-built nuclear ballistic missile submarine to enter service, and, a decade after the Americans, the first Soviet SSBN to mount the missiles within the hull (as opposed to in the fin). Since 1978 nine Yankees have had their missile section removed (the most recent being in 1982), thus shortening the hull by 95ft (28·9m), and they are now employed as SSNs. This conversion is required to keep the Soviet strategic missile strength within the limits agreed in SALT. Like the Soviet Echo-I class and the American Ethan Allen and Washington boats, such a conversion produces a useful addition to the SSN fleet but one which will inevitably fall short of the capabilities of a purpose-built attack submarine.

Victor Class

SSN (Soviet Union)

Fifteen boats + 3 building

Displacement: 5,000 tons surfaced; 6,000 tons submerged.
Dimensions: Length 337·9ft (103m); beam 32·8ft (10m); draught 23·9ft (7·3m).
Propulsion: Nuclear, 30,000shp; 1 shaft; 30kt dived.
Armament: SS-N-15/SS-NX-16 missiles; 6 21in (533mm) torpedo tubes.
Complement: 120.

First seen by Western observers in 1968, the Victor class is a second-generation Soviet nuclear-powered attack submarine. Somewhat shorter than the November class (qv), but with as great a beam, sixteen of the first type—Victor-I—were built. These were followed by the Victor-II, which is 15ft 3in (4·6m) longer to enable it to carry the SS-N-15 missile. Only six of these boats were built before production changed to yet another development, 11ft 6in (3·5m) longer still and with a cylindrical pod mounted on top of the upper rudder. This has subsequently been confirmed as the first Soviet towed sonar array, and it can be assumed that this device will be seen more widely on other attack submarines in future. Other

sensors are a large, low-frequency sonar array in the bow, and a medium-frequency array for torpedo control. It is also reported that Victor-III hulls are coated with the Soviet Clusterguard anechoic protection to attenuate the reflections which are returned to searching hostile warships. There are now fifteen Victor-IIIs in a class which will probably eventually number eighteen. A new class is expected to replace the Victor-III, the first of which should be at sea in 1984.

On 27 February 1982 the Italian Sauro class submarine *Leonardo da Vinci* detected a Soviet Victor-I at a depth of some 984ft (300m), 25 miles (40km) south-east of the naval base at Taranto. The Italians tracked the Soviet submarine for some 18 hours until it left Italian territorial waters. In reporting this incident the Italian authorities made it clear that this was by no means the first such incursion by a Soviet submarine. It is also noteworthy that the public announcement was absolutely positive about the nationality *and type* of the target, a rare acknowledgement of the precision of modern underwater identification technology.

Below: When first seen by Western observers the pod on the fin of the Victor-III caused some mystification. It has since been confirmed as a towed-array sonar and represents a sensible and neat way of stowing the device, which could well be copied in the West. The hull also has Clusterguard protection.

Valiant Class

SSN (UK)

Five boats

Displacement: 4,400 tons surfaced; 4,900 tons submerged.
Dimensions: Length 285ft (86·9m); beam 33·2ft (10·1m); draught 27ft (8·2m).
Propulsion: Nuclear, 15,000shp; 1 shaft; 25kt dived.
Armament: 6 21in (533mm) torpedo tubes.
Complement: 103.

The Royal Navy first studied the possibility of nuclear power for submarines in 1946, and in 1954 a naval section started work at the research station at Harwell. A land-based prototype submarine reactor went 'critical' in 1965, but a complete S5W was bought from the USA to power the first British nuclear submarine—HMS *Dreadnought*—which was launched in 1960. The bow section, containing the Type 2001 sonar, was of wholly British design and much blunter than the USS *Skipjack*'s. Unlike all later American SSNs, *Dreadnought* set the British style for retaining the foreplanes on the bow, rather than high on the fin. After many years service *Dreadnought* was put into reserve in 1982, but is unlikely ever to rejoin the fleet.

The first entirely British nuclear submarine, HMS *Valiant*, was ordered in August 1960 and completed in July 1966. Longer than *Dreadnought* by 19ft (5·8m) and with a somewhat larger complement, she is otherwise generally similar to her predecessor. Four more were built before production switched to the Swiftsure class (qv.). In 1967 *Valiant* gave a convincing demonstration of an SSN's capabilities when she travelled 10,000 miles (16,093km) submerged from Singapore to the UK in just 28 days.

In the South Atlantic War *Conqueror* became the first SSN to sink a hostile ship when she torpedoed the Argentine cruiser *General Belgrano* on 2 May 1982. *Belgrano*, in company with two destroyers, was on a sweep to the south of the Falklands when she was intercepted; the British submarine fired two torpedoes, both of which hit. The cruiser sank with considerable loss of life and the two destroyers carried out a series of depth-charge attacks on the SSN before returning to rescue survivors.

Left: HMS *Dreadnought* (S-101) was the Royal Navy's first nuclear-powered submarine, and at the time of her launch in 1960 it was thought that no further conventional-powered boats would be needed. The sleek, smooth lines of the hull and fin make an interesting comparison with her Soviet contemporaries.

Below: HMS *Conqueror* (S-48) is the only SSN in any navy to have sunk an enemy warship in anger: the *General Belgrano* in 1982. Following that she and two others of the class posed such a threat that the Argentine surface fleet was confined to the 12-mile coastal limit, a dramatic demonstration of naval power.

Swiftsure Class

SSN (UK)
Six boats

Displacement: 4,200 tons surfaced; 4,500 tons submerged.
Dimensions: Length 272ft (82·9m); beam 32·25ft (9·83m); draught 27ft (8·2m).
Propulsion: Nuclear, 15,000shp; 1 shaft; 30kt dived.
Armament: 5 21in (533mm) torpedo tubes.
Complement: 97.

The third class of British SSNs were the Swiftsures, the first of which joined the fleet in April 1973. These boats are 13ft (4m) longer than the Valiants (qv), with a flat upper deck which maintains the maximum diameter for a much greater length and gives a completely different shape from the 'humped back' of earlier British SSNs. This new shape is evidence of greater internal volume in the pressure hull, leading to more equipment space and better living conditions. The fin is not as tall as on the earlier classes, and the diving planes are set much lower and further forward (and are not, in fact, visible when the boat is on the surface). There are five torpedo tubes with twenty reloads, a heavy armament for the size of the hull. The torpedoes are the latest Tigerfish Mk 24 (Modified), and reload time is reported to be 15 seconds per tube.

Spartan and *Splendid* of this class took part in the 1982 South Atlantic War and, with the three *Valiant* class SSNs, were responsible for the blockade which effectively kept the Argentine Navy in port after the sinking of *Belgrano*. This episode demonstrated the value of the SSNs, and also showed how helpless a navy with limited ASW resources is against such a sophisticated threat.

Below: Six Swiftsure class SSNs have been built for the Royal Navy.

Trafalgar Class

SSN (UK)

One boat + 3 building

Displacement: 4,920 tons submerged.
Dimensions: Length 280ft (85·4m); hull diameter 32·25ft (9·83m).
Propulsion: Nuclear, 15,000shp; 1 shaft; 30+kt dived.
Armament: 5 21in (533mm) torpedo tubes.
Complement: Not known.

The next type of British SSN is the Trafalgar class, the first of which was launched on 1 July 1981 and commissioned on 27 May 1983. Four of these boats are on order with the possibility of a further two later. Little is known of the Trafalgar class except that they are a logical development of the Swiftsure design but the hull has been slightly stretched by including one more section in the parallel body, thus increasing overall length from 272ft (82 9m) to 280ft (85·4m). The diameter of the pressure hull remains unchanged at 32·25ft (9·83m), but there is an increase in submerged displacement to 4,920 tons. A new type of reactor core is used, and the machinery is mounted on rafts to insulate it from the hull and thus cut down radiated noise. There are five 21in (533mm) torpedo tubes, with twenty reloads.

The cost of these SSNs is a good indicator of the problem facing the major navies. At 1976 prices the building costs of the Swiftsure were: *Swiftsure* £37.1 million; *Superb* £41.3 million; *Sceptre* £58.9 million; and *Spartan* £68.9 million. The cost of the fourth Trafalgar submarine, including weapons systems and equipment, will be £175 million!

Below: A Vickers-produced cutaway of HMS *Trafalgar* showing the spacious hull of a modern SSN. The torpedo tubes are set back to free the bows for the largest possible sonar array.

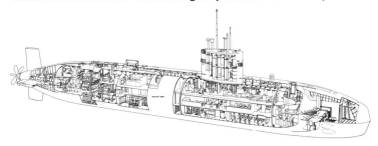

Below: HMS *Trafalgar*, first of the latest class of RN SSNs.

Los Angeles/Lipscomb Classes

SSN (USA)

Thirty + 20 building + 7 ordered/one boat

Displacement: 6,900 tons submerged.
Dimensions: Length 360ft (109·7m); beam 33ft (10·1m); draught 32·3ft (9·8m).
Propulsion: Nuclear, 35,000shp; 1 shaft; 30+kt dived.
Armament: Harpoon and Tomahawk missiles; SUBROC; 4 21in (533mm) torpedo tubes.
Complement: 127.
(Specifications given for Los Angeles class.)

Lipscomb was launched in 1973, the outcome of a development programme for a 'quiet' submarine stretching back to the *Tullibee* (qv) of the early 1960s. *Lipscomb* has many interesting features to achieve silent running, many of which have subsequently been incorporated into the Los Angeles class, although the turbo-electric plant, which removes the requirement for gearing (the prime source of noise in SSNs), was not. *Lipscomb* is still in front-line service.

The first Los Angeles class SSN entered service in 1976; thirty are now in commission, twenty are under construction and a further seven are on order, making this one of the most massive and expensive defence programmes undertaken by any nation. The Los Angeles boats are much larger than any previous US Navy SSN and have a higher submerged speed. They have the very long-range BQQ-5 sonar and the BQS-15 short-range system, and also operate towed arrays. Weapons fits can include SUBROC, Harpoon and Tomahawk, as well as conventional and wire-guided torpedoes. Thus, like all other US SSNs, although they are primarily intended to hunt and destroy other submarines and to protect SSBNs, the Los Angeles submarines can also be used without modification to sink surface ships at long range, while Tomahawk will enable them to attack strategic targets well inland. The BQQ-5 sonar is particularly effective, and is reported on one occasion to have enabled an American SSN to track two Soviet Victor class (qv) SSNs simultaneously.

The Los Angeles class is very sophisticated and each boat is an extremely potent fighting machine; moreover, with a production run of at least 57 boats it must be considered a very successful design. Nevertheless, the class is also becoming very expensive: in 1976 the cost of each boat was estimated at $221·25 million, but the boat bought in FY79 cost $325·6 million and the two in FY81 $495·8 million each. Not even the USA can continue to spend money at that rate.

Below: The launch of a Los Angeles class SSN illustrates the size of these vessels. These are the most effective of all nuclear-powered attack submarines, with ASW sensors and weapons, anti-ship missiles and strategic cruise missiles, enabling them to carry out a variety of important naval functions.

Below: USS *Atlanta* (SSN-712). At least 57 of these boats are to be built, with current costs running at $US495·8 million per unit, making this possibly the most expensive defence programme ever. The Los Angeles class is designed to protect US carrier groups and attack Soviet SSBNs, both vital tasks.

Sturgeon/Narwhal Classes

SSN (USA)

Thirty-seven/one boat

Displacement: 3,640 tons surfaced; 4,640 tons submerged.
Dimensions: Length 292·2ft (89m); beam 31·7ft (9·7m); draught 26ft (7·9m).
Propulsion: Nuclear, 15,000shp; 1 shaft; 20+kt dived.
Armament: SUBROC; 4 21in (533mm) torpedo tubes.
Complement: 107.
(Specifications given for Sturgeon class).

The 37 Sturgeon class SSNs are slightly larger and improved versions of the Permit design. They have an Albacore-type hull with the four torpedo tubes amidships to clear the bow for the BQQ-2 sonar system, and can be distinguished from the earlier class by the taller sail with diving planes set lower down to facilitate control at periscope depth; these diving planes

can be rotated to the vertical when surfacing through ice. There were several problems during building this class: one boat had to be moved to another yard to be completed, while another sank in 35ft (10·7m) of water while fitting out—an incident described by the US Congress as 'wholly avoidable'.

To reduce noise the Sturgeons are fitted with two contra-rotating propellers. Although American SSNs are already very quiet, anything which can be done to reduce the noise signature is speedily introduced and tested by the US Navy. An experimental SSN, based on the *Permit,* is *Narwhal,* built to test the S5G free-circulation reactor, which has no pumps and is, therefore, quieter than previous US reactors. However, whilst *Narwhal* retains this system and is still in service, no further submarines have been built with such a system.

The last nine boats of the Sturgeon class were built 10ft (3m) longer to accommodate additional sonar and electronic gear and all boats in the class will have their BQQ-2 sonar replaced by the latest BQQ-5 equipment in the course of routine refits. Most are already fitted to fire either Harpoon or Tomahawk, and all carry SUBROC and anti-submarine torpedoes.

Left: USS *Bergall* (SSN-667): a dramatic shot of an emergency surfacing drill, which allows a rare glimpse of the bow profile of a US SSN. By positioning the torpedo tubes amidships US designers have been able to put a massive sonar array in the bow.

Below: USS *Tunny* (SSN-682) underway in the Atlantic, showing the great length of these US SSNs, which, combined with their large diameter, gives vast internal volume. All Sturgeons are to have their BQQ-2 sonar replaced by the BQQ-5 during refits to bring them to the same standard as the Los Angeles class.

Permit (Thresher)/Tullibee Classes

SSN (USA)

Thirteen/one boat

Displacement: 3,750 tons surfaced; 4,300 tons submerged.
Dimensions: Length 278·5ft (84·9m); beam 31·7ft (9·6m); draught 28·4ft (8·7m).
Propulsion: Nuclear, 15,000shp; 1 shaft; 20+kt dived.
Armament: Sub-Harpoon missiles; SUBROC; 4 21in (533mm) torpedo tubes.
Complement: 103.
(Specifications given for Permit class).

One of the smallest SSNs, *Tullibee* (2,640 tons submerged) was an early attempt to build the ideal hunter-killer submarine. The torpedo tubes were fitted amidships for the first time, to free the bows for the then-new BQQ-2 conformal sonar array. *Tullibee* is very manoeuvrable and is fitted with turbo-electric drive to eliminate the noise made by the reduction gears in earlier SSNs. However, small size also meant low submerged speed and lack of space, and no more SSNs of this size have been built for the US Navy. *Tullibee* remains in service but is no longer a first-line unit.

The better features of *Tullibee* were incorporated into the Thresher class, which, after the loss of the name-ship in the Atlantic in April 1963, was redesignated the Permit class; the boats were built between 1960 and 1966. Four were originally designed to take the Regulus II cruise missile but were reordered as SSNs when Regulus was cancelled in favour of Polaris. The last three of this class (SSN614, 615 and 621) have a larger hull, whilst *Jack* (SSN605) was modified to take contra-rotating propellers in one of the US Navy's many attempts to find a really quiet propulsion system.

The principal anti-submarine weapon in this class is SUBROC, which is controlled by the BQQ-2 sonar system, and the anti-ship Harpoon missile can also be fired. Refits to take the Tomahawk SLCM and the BQQ-5 sonar will be undertaken in due course.

Below: USS *Tullibee* (SSN-597) was an experimental design whose best features were incorporated into the Permit design.

Above: USS *Permit* (SSN-594) showing the excellent hydrodynamic features of her hull, fin and diving-plane design.

Below: USS *Guardfish* (SSN-612) of the Permit class has four 21in (533mm) torpedo tubes amidships, angled at 10°.

Skipjack Class

SSN (USA)

Five boats

Displacement: 3,075 tons surfaced; 3,513 tons submerged.
Dimensions: Length 251·7ft (76·6m); beam 31·5ft (9·6m); draught 29·4ft (8·9m).
Propulsion: Nuclear, 15,000shp; 1 shaft; 30+kt dived.
Armament: 6 21in (533mm) torpedo tubes.
Complement: 93.

The Skipjack class SSNs were the first nuclear submarines to incorporate the teardrop-shaped hull developed by the conventionally powered USS *Albacore,* which raised submerged speeds from some 20+kt to well over 30. Underwater manoeuvrability is also much improved, though the use of only one propeller brings its own problems and means that a stern torpedo tube can no longer be fitted.

One of the first of this class, *Scorpion* (SSN589), was modified on the slip to become the first of the George Washington class SSBNs. A second Scorpion was then built from scratch, but this was lost in the Atlantic south of the Azores in May 1968. The five other Skipjacks remain in service.

All engine fittings in the Skipjacks are duplicated (except for the reactor and the propeller) to minimise the danger of a breakdown. The boats have had their original sonar equipment updated but BQQ-5 will not be fitted because the torpedo tubes are in the old bow position. It can be assumed that these boats (which were the first class to use the S5W nuclear reactor) and the even older three remaining Skate class boats will soon reach the end of their useful lives.

Below: USS *Scamp* (SSN-588) of the Skipjack class. This was the first SSN design to utilise the Albacore hull, a teardrop shape which increases speed and manoeuvrability, as well as maximising internal volume. *Scorpion* (SSN-589) was lost in the Atlantic in May 1968, taking the lives of 99 crew members.

Ethan Allen Class

SSN (USA)
Five boats

Displacement: 6,955 tons surfaced; 7,880 tons submerged.
Dimensions: Length 410ft (125m); beam 33ft (10·1m); draught 32ft (9·8m).
Propulsion: Nuclear, 15,000shp; 1 shaft; 30kt dived.
Armament: 4 21in (533mm) torpedo tubes.
Complement: 142.
(Specifications given for Ethan Allen class).

George Washington (SSBN598), one of the few truly historic submarines, was laid down as *Scorpion* (SSN589) but was lengthened by the addition of a 130ft (40m) insert while on the stocks to become the first SSBN. She was followed by four more vessels, and these introduced the whole concept of the undersea, virtually invulnerable nuclear deterrent. Two of the class (*Roosevelt* and *Lincoln*) had their missile compartments removed in 1980, and the spent fuel was disposed of. The bow and stern sections of the hull were then rejoined, but the two decommissioned hulks are now being cannibalised for spares prior to disposal. The remaining three boats are being converted to SSNs by the removal of the missiles and associated equipment; cement will then be put in the missile tubes as ballast compensation. The cost of this conversion is a mere $400,000 per boat, and the three will then be used for ASW training for some three years until their nuclear cores reach the end of their current life, thus releasing more modern SSNs for front-line duties.

The Ethan Allens were the first to be specifically designed for the SSBN role and although generally similar to the Washington class they are nearly 30ft (9·1m) longer. They were upgraded to take the Polaris A-3 SLBM but will not be converted further to take Poseidon missiles; instead, all five are being converted into SSNs and will operate in the attack role until the end of the 1980s at least. This conversion parallels that being carried out by the Soviet Navy with its Yankee class SSBNs.

Below: USS *Thomas A Edison* (SSN-610), one of the Ethan Allen SSBNs which have now been converted to SSNs by placing cement blocks in the missile tubes and removing missile-related systems.

Conventional Submarines (SSK)

In the early 1950s it was forecast that all future submarines in the major navies would be nuclear-powered. However, things have turned out somewhat differently, and diesel-electric submarines are found in almost every fleet, only the US Navy having attained a virtual all-nuclear status (although the French recently committed themselves to such a goal). The Soviet Union retains several hundred conventional boats in service and is producing many more every year. The modern conventional submarine has advantages to offer, not least economy. The two Los Angeles class SSNs constructed in FY81 cost $495.8 million each; these are sophisticated, deep-ocean boats, but few navies can afford costs of that order. SSNs also require large crews (*Los Angeles* 127, *Swiftsure* 97) compared to diesel-electric boats (Type 209 33, Type 2400 46).

Nuclear submarines are very powerful and fast (over 40kt in some cases), and their endurance is only really limited by crew fatigue. SSNs cannot, however avoid making some noise, which renders them liable to detection, particularly within the confines of the continental shelf. Conventional boats are much quieter when running on their electric motors, and therefore more suitable for ASW patrol, reconnaissance and clandestine missions. Excellent examples of the last were afforded by the Soviet Whiskey class boat which ran aground in Swedish territorial waters in late 1981, and by the British *Onyx* which delivered SAS and SBS patrols to the Falkland Islands in the 1982 war.

Conventional submarine development is now at a critical stage, with many existing types in numerous navies becoming due for replacement, especially the ex-US Guppy types, the British Porpoises and Oberons and the Soviet Whiskeys and Romeos. There are several types either in the design stage or in production, of which the German and French have been the most successful so far. The British Type 2400 is undoubtedly the most sophisticated of these designs and will probably be the most combat-effective and versatile, although it may also prove far too expensive for most navies. For once, the USA has totally opted out of this field and finds itself with absolutely nothing to offer.

Modern conventional submarines fall into three categories. The first is the 400–600-ton coastal boat such as the German Type 205/206 and the Italian Toti class. These are effective in their way, but suffer from limitations in range, torpedo reloads and sensor capacity. The next size is the 900–1,300-ton group, for example the German Type 209, the Yugoslavian *Sava* and the Swedish Näcken and Sjöormen classes. These, too, are limited in endurance and carrying capacity and are to be found in the smaller navies with medium-range roles. The majority of current types lie in the 1,600+ ton category (Japanese *Uzushio*, British Type 2400, Dutch *Walrus*, Soviet Foxtrot), with the Soviet Tango class of 3,700 tons at the top end.

Below: Spanish Navy's *Delfin* (French Daphné class) on trials in 1973.

Agosta Class

SSK (France)

Ten boats

Displacement: 1,450 tons surfaced; 1,725 tons submerged.
Dimensions: Length 221·7ft (67·6m); beam 22·3ft (6·8m); draught 17·7ft (5·4m).
Propulsion: 2 diesel, 3,600bhp; 1 electric, 4,600hp; 1 shaft; 20kt dived.
Armament: 4 21in (533mm) torpedo tubes.
Complement: 52.

Agosta, name ship of the class, joined the French fleet in July 1977 and was followed by three more in 1977–78, completing the French Navy's own order. A further four Agostas have been built in Spain by Bazan and two have been built in France for the Pakistani Navy. The South Africans wanted to order two as well, but this was blocked for political reasons. Egypt was interested at one time in purchasing two Agostas, but no order has ever been announced.

Somewhat larger than the previous Daphnés, the Agosta class is intended for distant-water operation. Only four torpedo tubes are fitted, but there are twenty reloads and special devices for rapid reloading. The tubes are 21in (533mm) in diameter, the first time that the French have abandoned their previous 21·7in (550mm); this is presumably intended to enhance the export potential of the type. ASW equipment includes a passive sonar set (DSUV-2) with 36 microphones, two active sets, and a passive ranging set under a spiky dome on the foredeck. Great attention has been devoted to silent running, and an unusual feature is the fitting of a small 30hp electric motor for very quiet, low-speed movement whilst on patrol.

If the French Navy sticks to its announced intention to concentrate on nuclear-powered submarines in future, the Agosta class could be the last of a distinguished and interesting line of French conventional boats.

Below: *Agosta* (S620) nameship of a class of four in service with the French Navy; a further six serve in foreign fleets. This design is exceptionally quiet and was used as the basis for the SNA72, France's first SSNs.

Daphné Class

SSK (France)
Twenty-two boats

Displacement: 869 tons surfaced; 1,043 tons submerged.
Dimensions: Length 189·6ft (57·8m); beam 22·3ft (6·8m); draught 15·1ft (4·6m).
Propulsion: 3 diesel, 1,300bhp; 2 electric, 1,600hp; 2 shafts; 16kt dived.
Armament: 12 21·7in (550mm) torpedo tubes.
Complement: 45.

In the late 1940s the French Navy had some fourteen types of submarine in service, ranging from ocean-going types to 'midgets'. One of the former was an ex-German Type XXI taken over in 1945, and this design was then improved and produced in France as the Narval class; six were built in the early 1950s, were rebuilt in the 1960s, and are still in service.

Next to appear was the Aréthuse class, small (669 tons submerged) hunter/killers, of which four were built; one (*Argonaute*) remains in service with two in reserve. In the following Daphné class, careful attention was paid to silence of operation, and the exterior shape of the hull was tested in great detail. All mooring equipment is retractable and there are even microphones around the hull to monitor noise levels, the speed or manoeuvres of the boat capable of being adjusted accordingly.

Twenty Daphnés were built in France (French Navy 11, South Africa 3, Pakistan 3, Portugal 3) and a further four in Spain. Two mysterious losses (*Minerve* in 1968 and *Eurydice* in 1971) were nearly followed by a third in 1971 when the schnorkel sprang a leak due to a faulty valve, but on this occasion an alert captain took immediate remedial action and saved his boat. There have been no further losses, but neither have there been any more orders.

Below: *Daphné* (S641). A good design, which has sold well, but which acquired a bad reputation owing to two losses (in 1968 and 1971) due to valve faults in the schnorkel system. Microphones are fitted around the hull for self-monitoring of noise.

Type 209 Class

SSK (Germany, FDR)

Thirty-seven boats + ? building

Displacement: 1,100 tons surfaced; 1,210 tons submerged. See text.
Dimensions: Length 178·4ft (54·4m); beam 20·3ft (6·2m); draught 17·9ft (5·5m). See text.
Propulsion: 4 MTU diesel, 7,040KW; 1 Siemens electric, 3,070KW; 1 shaft; 23kt dived.
Armament: 8 21in (533mm) torpedo tubes.
Complement: 33.

Right: *U-29,* **a Type 206 SSK of the Federal Germany Navy. These boats are built of a specially-developed high-tensile non-magnetic steel, a feature unique to the German Navy. Underwater displacement of 498 tons was just within the limits then stipulated by the Allies.**

Below: A Type 209 built for export flies the Federal German ensign while on maker's trials. Two such boats in the Argentine Navy constituted a major threat to the British Task Force during the South Atlantic War of 1982.

Germany has a special place in the history of the submarine, ending World War II with some outstanding designs which, fortunately for the Allies, failed to attain operational status in significant numbers. It was not until 1954 that Germany was allowed to construct the Type 205, a small coastal boat, twelve of which were built for use in the Baltic. Two improved Type 205s were built in Denmark (Narvhalen class), and a further fifteen improved Type 205s, optimised for deep diving, were built in Germany for Norway as Type 207s.

Having completed the Type 205s, design work started on a follow-on class of 450-ton boats, the main concern being with greater battery power to meet the demands of the ever-increasing numbers of electrical and electronic devices but without reducing submerged speed or endurance. Construction of the first boat (*U-13*) began in November 1969, and the eighteenth and last joined the Bundesmarine in September 1971. Made of special non-magnetic steel, these submarines have served the German Navy well and, so far as is known, have totally avoided the notorious corrosion problems that affected the earlier Type 205s. The opportunity was taken in this class to upgrade the active and passive sonars and the fire-control system, and wire-guided torpedoes were fitted for the first time in a German submarine design.

The British Vickers Shipbuilding Group constructed three submarines for Israel under licence from Ingenieurkontor Lübeck (IKL) but fitted with British weapons systems. Described variously as an adaptation of the Type

206 or as a smaller Type 209, the IKL 540 is optimised for operations in the warmer waters of the eastern Mediterranean. A unique fitting is the fin-mounted SLAM, a quadruple Blowpipe SAM installation, giving the Israeli submarines an anti-aircraft capability.

Raising the Allied-imposed displacement limit on German submarine construction to 1,000 tons led to the design of the very successful Type 209, which has met the need of many navies for a new submarine, conventionally armed and powered but with up-to-date sensors and electronics and with minimal demands on highly skilled manpower. Operators include Greece (eight Type IK 36), Argentina (two IK 68), Peru (two IK 62 with 35-man crews), Colombia (two IK 78 with 35-man crews and Turkey (two IK 14 with 35-man crews). An improved version (IK 81), longer, and with a larger detection dome, has been ordered by Venezuela (4), Ecuador (2), Turkey (1), Greece (4), Peru (6) and Indonesia (4). Turkey, having received three from Howaldtswerke, is now producing her own; two have been completed so far, and another eight are planned.

The Type 209 is similar in shape and layout to the Type 205 but has increased dimensions, greater battery capacity and more powerful propulsion. The hull is completely smooth, with retractable hydroplanes mounted low on the bows, cruciform after control surfaces and a single screw. Careful hull design and powerful motors result in a staggering underwater 'burst' speed of 23kt. Designed for patrols of up to 50 days, these boats are armed with eight 21in (533mm) torpedo tubes and have a full range of sensors. They are one of the most successful contemporary submarine designs, and during the 1982 South Atlantic War the Royal Navy treated the two Argentine Type 209s with the greatest respect, although it is not clear whether the two boats actually went to sea. IKL has obviously assessed potential customers' requirements with remarkable accuracy.

Enrico Toti/Nazario Sauro Classes

SSK (Italy)

Four/four boats

Displacement: 524 tons surfaced; 582 tons submerged.
Dimensions: Length 151·5ft (46·2m); beam 15·4ft (4·7m); draught 13·1ft (4m).
Propulsion: 2 diesel, 2,200bhp; 1 electric, 2,200hp; 1 shaft; 15kt dived.
Armament: 4 21in (533mm) torpedo tubes.
Complement: 26.
(Specifications given for Enrico Toti class).

The postwar Italian Navy started with three wartime submarines (two Flutto and one Acciaio class), and five modernised Gato and Balao class were acquired from the USA. Although good, sound designs—especially following modernisation—these ex-US boats are somewhat large for the particular conditions found in the Mediterranean.

The operational requirement for the first indigenous postwar submarine—the Toti class—changed several times, and the design had to be recast accordingly before being finalised as a coastal hunter/killer. Built like all other Italian submarines at the Italcantieri yard at Montfalcone, the Totis are intended for the shallow, confined waters of the central Mediterranean and Adriatic; their restricted surface range is no handicap and enabled the size to be kept to a minimum. They are small and highly manoeuvrable, with a 'teardrop' hull and a single screw; they have diesel-electric drive, and maximum diving depth is some 600ft (180m). The JP64 active sonar is in a prominent dome in the bow, with the passive sonar beneath it in the stem, and the four torpedo tubes are also mounted in the bow. The class makes an interesting comparison with the German Types 205 and 206 (qv), and it is noteworthy that the Italian design has never won any export orders.

The Nazario Sauro class are the largest submarines produced in Italy since World War II, although at 1,630 tons submerged they are still somewhat smaller than the ex-US boats they are replacing. The hull is an Albacore-type 'teardrop' shape, with cruciform after control surfaces and a very large, slow-turning, seven-bladed propeller. The forward control surfaces are mounted, US-fashion, on the fin.

The Sauro class have six bow-mounted torpedo tubes with six reloads, and this total of twelve torpedoes seems inadequate for a large boat designed for 45-day patrols. The French Agosta class (qv), with a similar size and displacement, carries 16 reloads for its four tubes—a total of twenty torpedoes.

Many navies are looking for replacements for their conventional submarines in the 1,000-2,000-ton displacement range, but whereas orders have been placed for the German Type 209, the French Agosta and the Dutch Zwaardvis designs, none has yet been placed for the Sauro. Most noteworthy is the fact that when Greece and Turkey were looking for submarines to use in the Mediterranean they selected the Type 209 in preference to the Sauro (which had presumably been optimised for just those conditions).

Top right: *Lazzaro Mocenigo* (S-514) of the Enrico Toti class. The massive dome on the bow houses a JP-64 active sonar; the passive element is below it in the stem.

Right: *Nazario Sauro* (S-518) nameship of a class of four built in the late 1970s. Although optimised for the Mediterranean, other navies in the area have bought foreign boats.

Yuushio Class

SSK (Japan)

Five boats + 1 building

Displacement: 2,200 tons surfaced.
Dimensions: Length 249·3ft (76m); beam 32·5ft (9·9m); draught 24·6ft (7·5m).
Propulsion: 2 diesel, 4,200bhp; 1 electric, 7,200hp; 1 shaft; 20kt dived.
Armament: 6 21in (533mm) torpedo tubes.
Complement: 75

The Japanese Maritime Self-Defense Force (JMSDF) produced its first indigenous postwar submarine design in 1959 and a second, improved class in 1961-62. All these boats have now been stricken, but the culmination of this line—the four boats of the Asashio class—is still in service. This is a neat and workmanlike design, with the now somewhat rare feature of twin 12·7in (322mm) stern torpedo tubes, which are feasible only because of the twin propellers.

The next class—Uzushio—was based on a US Navy design, with an Albacore-type 'teardrop' hull for faster and quieter underwater performance. The hull is of very high quality steel to permit a diving depth of up to 650ft (220m). Seven of the class are in service.

The latest Japanese submarines are those of the Yuushio class, an all-round improvement on the Uzushio class and capable of slightly higher speeds. Both the Uzushio and Yuushio submarines have their torpedo tubes mounted amidships, firing outwards at an angle of 10° to the hull, a feature they share with the US Navy's SSNs. This is done in order to free the entire bow area for a large sonar array. The Uzushio class have pressure hulls of high-tensile steel (NS-63), permitting a diving depth of some 1,970ft (600m). The Yuushios, however, use even more modern steel (NS-90), giving a claimed diving depth of some 3,280ft (1,000m). The first two Yuushios will be retrospectively fitted with Sub-Harpoon missiles,

Below: *Isoshio* of the JMSDF Uzushio class. Built 1968-75, the seven boats of this class preceded the latest Yuushio class.

Above: *Mochishio* of the Yuushio class looks like an SSN, but is, in fact, a conventional diesel-electric submarine.

but the remaining boats of the class are being fitted with these missiles prior to delivery. A noteworthy feature of these Japanese submarines is their large complements, much greater for the size of hull than in other navies.

These Japanese submarines are very advanced, as would be expected from such a technologically capable nation, and would seem to be fully equivalent to SSNs in most features except that of underwater endurance. This may be encouraging the JMSDF to seek a solution to the problem of freeing the non-nuclear submarine from the necessity of having to come up to the surface to 'breathe' at regular intervals.

The role of these Japanese submarines in war would be to defend Japanese waters from incursions by foreign (presumably Soviet) surface and underwater vessels. It may be assumed that this would include patrols in the Sea of Okhotsk, which is a known haven for Soviet SSBNs.

Dolfijn Class

SSK (Netherlands)

Four boats

Displacement: 1,494 tons surfaced; 1,826 tons submerged.
Dimensions: Length 260·9ft (79·5m); beam 25·8ft (7·8m); draught 16·4ft (5m).
Propulsion: 2 diesel, 3,100bhp; 2 electric, 4,200hp; 2 shafts; 17kt dived.
Armament: 8 21in (533mm) (4 bow, 4 stern) torpedo tubes.
Complement: 67.

The Dutch Navy has a reputation for innovative submarine design: it was, for example, a Dutch naval officer who invented the schnorkel tube in the mid-1930s. It is thus not surprising that it has come up with an unusual, indeed unique, concept for its first postwar class of four boats, authorised in 1949. The first pair (*Dolfijn* and *Zeehond*) were not laid down until 1954, and the second pair (*Potvis* and *Tonjin*) were delayed pending a decision on whether they should be nuclear-powered. Finally realising that this would be prohibitively expensive, the last two boats were laid down in 1962 and completed in 1965–66. Naturally this second pair incorporated improvements and were for some time considered to be a separate class. Since then, however, various refits have led to all four boats being virtually identical again.

The outstanding feature of this class is that they have three separate but interconnected pressure hulls in a 'treble-bubble' arrangement. The larger, upper hull contains the crew and most of the equipment, whilst below it and alongside each other are two smaller hulls containing machinery and stores. The advantage of this layout is that it gives increased strength and compactness, allowing a permitted diving depth of 980ft (300m). Conditions in the two lower hulls are, however, very cramped, making machinery maintenance and repair very difficult; this, allied to general complexity and manufacturing costs, dissuaded the Dutch from developing this interesting idea any further. The streamlined outer hull gives an excellent underwater performance and these are very quiet boats. The two oldest in the class will be paid off when the two new Walrus class submarines join the fleet.

Below: *Potvis* (S804). The outer hull disguises the unique treble-bubble pressure hull which confers great strength.

Zwaardvis/Walrus Classes

SSK (Netherlands)
Two boats/two building

Displacement: 2,350 tons surfaced; 2,640 tons submerged.
Dimensions: Length 217·2ft (66·2m); beam 33·8ft (10·3m); draught 23·3ft (7·1m).
Propulsion: 3 diesel, 5,200bhp; 1 electric; 1 shaft; 20kt dived.
Armament: 6 21in (533mm) torpedo tubes.
Complement: 65.
(Specifications given for Zwaardvis class; see text for Walrus class variations).

The two boats of the Zwaardvis class are among the largest conventional submarines currently in service, matched only by the US Barbel, the Soviet Tango and the projected British Type 2400 classes. The design of the Zwaardvis does, in fact, owe a great deal to the Barbel, with a similar Albacore hull, giving considerable internal depth and making it possible to incorporate two decks. This gives a generally roomy interior, which has great advantages for living conditions. Three diesel generators power the propulsion motor for surface running and two groups of batteries provide underwater power. A single, five-bladed propeller is mounted abaft the cruciform control surfaces, and a 'burst' speed in excess of 20kt has been reported.

The Zwaardvis boats will be supplemented in the late 1980s by two improved submarines designated the Walrus class. The dimensions and silhouettes are virtually identical, but use of the new French 'Marel' high-tension steel will increase diving depth by at least 50 per cent in the new vessels. An updated and automated fire control and command system (codenamed 'Gipsy') will allow a reduction in complement from 65 to 49, a very significant factor in such a small navy. The two boats so far ordered will replace the *Dolfijn* and *Zeehond* in the late 1980s, and two more are planned to replace *Potvis* and *Tonjin* in the early 1990s.

These Dutch submarines are capable of protracted operations in the Atlantic, where they would operate as part of the task groups which the Royal Netherlands Navy has undertaken to provide as part of its NATO commitment.

Below: The conventionally-powered Zwaardvis-class submarine *Tijgerhaai* (S807); note the high-speed, teardrop hull form.

Tango/Kilo Classes

SSK (Soviet Union)

Seventeen/two boats

Displacement: 3,000 tons surfaced; 3,700 tons submerged.
Dimensions: Length 301·8ft (92m); beam 29·5ft (9m); draught 23ft (7m).
Propulsion: 3 diesel, 6,000bhp; 3 electric, 6,000hp; 3 shafts; 16kt dived.
Armament: 8 21in (533mm) torpedo tubes.
Complement: 62.
(Specifications given for Tango class.)

The Soviet Navy has a vast fleet of conventional submarines: at least 200 are currently in service, with a further 100 in reserve. Some fifty Whiskey-V boats are in service, and it was one of these that ran aground near the Swedish naval base at Karlskrona in 1982. The next class was the Romeo, an improved Whiskey, of which 560 were initially planned although this was cut back to twenty when the nuclear fleet was expanded. Some sixty of the Foxtrot class are in service, built between 1958 and 1971 for the Soviet Navy although small scale production continues for export.

The Tango class was first seen by Western observers at the Sebastopol Naval Review in July 1973, and production has continued ever since at a rate of some 2–3 boats per year. This class is of advanced design, and it is of interest that the Soviet Union does not seem particularly keen to export it, despite the considerable market for a conventionally-powered submarine of this size and capability. It is clearly regarded as complementary to the SSNs, and could well be intended for use in the extensive shallow waters around the Soviet Union. The continued production of this class, and of the later Kilo as well, makes it clear that the Soviets do not intend to follow the US lead in aiming for an all-nuclear submarine fleet.

Above: Tango class SSK—3,700 tons submerged displacement—currently the largest non-nuclear submarine class in service.

The hull of the Tango class has very smooth lines, but one noteworthy feature is that forward of the fin there is a marked rise of some 3ft (0·91m). This will undoubtedly improve seakeeping qualities on the surface, but also suggests a requirement for extra volume in the forward end of the boat, possibly for some new weapon system; it has also been reported that the latest boats have a slightly longer hull to allow for a new weapon to be fitted. The smooth lines of these submarines suggest a small and compact design, but this is deceptive as they are, in fact, the largest conventional submarines currently in production.

First reported from the Far East in 1981 is the successor to the Whiskey and Romeo—the Kilo class. These boats are in production at the Komsomolsk Navy Yard and entered service with the Soviet Pacific Fleet in 1983; they are expected to deploy with Western hemisphere fleets in 1984. Early estimates are that the Kilo has a displacement of some 2,500 tons on the surface and 3,200 tons submerged. It would thus seem to be about the same size as the Tango class, from which it has probably been developed.

Below: Tango class diesel-electric submarine of the Soviet Navy. The unusual rise in the bow lines can be seen in this picture, a feature which is thought to house a new weapon system. The follow-on Kilo class is now entering service.

Sjöormen/Näcken Classes

SSK (Sweden)
Five/three boats

Displacement: 1,030 tons surfaced; 1,125 tons submerged.
Dimensions: Length 162·4ft (49·5m); beam 18·4ft (5·6m); draught 18·4ft (5·6m).
Propulsion: 2 diesel, 2,200bhp; 1 electric; 1 shaft; 20kt dived.
Armament: 6 21in (533mm) and 2 16in (406mm) torpedo tubes.
Complement: 19.
(Specifications given for Näcken class; see text for details of Sjöorman class).

Sweden's first submarine was launched in 1904 and since then there has been a succession of small but efficient boats, designed primarily for use in the Baltic. The five submarines of the Sjöormen class joined the Swedish fleet between 1967 and 1969. The design was based, like so many others at that time, on the revolutionary Albacore hull, as were the indexed cruciform after control surfaces. The large fin towers over the bow and the forward control surfaces are mounted on the fin rather than on the bows, in line with American practice. Endurance is estimated to be some 21 days, and the class is intended for operations in the very tricky Baltic waters. The crew normally numbers 23, although operation with a mere 18 is possible for short periods.

The Sjöormens were followed in the late 1970s by the Näcken class. These boats can operate at depths of up to 984ft (300m) and may well be intended to deploy outside the Baltic in the deep trenches of the Skagerrak. Based on the Sjöormen, the Näcken is a little smaller, and very great attention has been paid to quietness and to effective control at slow speeds. Although the third Näcken class boat was commissioned in 1979, it is possible that two more may be built before the first of a new type—the A17—is laid down. Little is known of the A17 except that it is being designed by Kockums of Malmö.

Below: *Sjöhästen,* one of five boats of the Royal Swedish Navy's Sjöormen class, designed specifically for Baltic operations.

Upholder (Type 2400) Class

SSK (UK)

Not yet building

Displacement: 2,125 tons surfaced; 2,362 tons submerged.
Dimensions: Length 230·5ft (70·25m); beam 24·9ft (7·6m); draught 24·6ft (7·5m).
Propulsion: 2 diesel; 1 electric; 1 shaft; 20+kt dived.
Armament: 6 21in (533mm) torpedo tubes.
Complement: 46.

It was once intended that the Oberon class would be the last conventional boats for the Royal Navy. It is now, however, accepted that, although the nuclear-powered submarine has many advantages, there is still an operational need for the conventional type as well. There is thus an urgent need to replace the Porpoise and Oberon boats since the hulls are all over 20 years old and, more importantly, the design itself is based on the technology of the early 1950s. The new RN patrol submarine (SSK-01) will be based very closely upon the Vickers Type 2400, so called because its submerged displacement is 2,400 metric tonnes (2,362 tons). This type will be built at a rate of about one per year and will be a very welcome addition to the fleet. A unit cost of £50 million has been quoted, but it would seem probable that it will be very much more.

The new class will have a 'teardrop' type hull with cruciform after hydroplanes and retractable forward hydroplanes mounted low on the bow; the RN has never accepted the US mountings on the fin. Many special features have been incorporated into the design to minimise radiated noise and thus achieve a marked reduction in the noise signature. A major factor is the maximum use of labour-saving devices, thus reducing the crew to 46 compared to 69 in the Oberons. A diesel-electric propulsion system, comprising a single fixed-pitch propeller on a shaft directly driven by a twin-armature electric motor, is fitted. On the surface, and when 'snorting', two four-stroke high-speed diesels are used, each driving a 1·25MW AC generator. The most modern sensors will be fitted, and there will be six torpedo tubes in the bow. These will fire normal torpedoes or Harpoon missiles, or can be used to lay mines.

There is a large overseas market for this type and size of patrol submarine with countries who want to replace their Oberons, Guppies and Balaos, and the Type 2400 is already on offer to Australia and Canada.

Below: The Royal Navy's future class of conventional submarines (SSK) will be built by Vickers—the Upholder (Type 2400) class. They will be extremely sophisticated boats with a capacious hull, as shown clearly in this cutaway drawing. The twin-deck layout will allow plenty of room for sensors, weapons and crew, while the setting back of the torpedo tubes will leave ample space for a large sonar array in the bow. Careful design and the extensive use of labour-saving devices has limited the crew required to 46, a feature of particular interest to small navies.

Porpoise/Oberon Classes

SSK (UK)

Three/twenty-seven boats

Displacement: 2,030 tons surfaced; 2,410 tons submerged.
Dimensions: Length 295·2ft (90m); beam 26·5ft (8·1m); draught 18ft (5·5m).
Propulsion: 2 diesel, 3,680bhp; 2 electric, 6,000hp; 2 shafts; 17kt dived.
Armament: 8 21in (533mm) (6 bow, 2 stern) torpedo tubes.
Complement: 71/69.

Right: HMS *Porpoise* (S01) is the Royal Navy's oldest submarine; she was launched in 1956.

Below right: HMS *Osiris* (S13), launched in November 1962, is one of the RN's ageing fleet of 16 diesel-electric submarines.

Below: HMS *Orpheus* (S11), an Oberon class submarine, entering harbour. A successful design which has sold well abroad, these boats are now overdue for replacement by the Upholder class.

After the end of the World War II the Royal Navy ran trials with a number of ex-German submarines, which included HMS *Meteorite* (ex-*U-1407*), one of the Walther Type XVIIBs powered by a hydrogen-peroxide fuelled engine. This was followed by two British-designed and built hydrogen-peroxide boats (*Explorer* and *Excalibur*), which were tested in 1956–65 when—to the profound relief of their crews—the project was abandoned.

The first British postwar submarines to reach operational status were the Porpoise class, which combined the best features of conventional British and German wartime designs and which also owed more than a little to the design of the USS *Tang*. The Porpoise boats have a semi-streamlined hull and are extremely quiet, with excellent range and habitability, and have a deep designed diving depth of 800–900ft (244–275m). Some of the class were stricken before the planned date to permit more men and money to be devoted to the Royal Navy's nuclear submarine programme, but three boats remain in service.

The Oberon class is a virtual repeat of the Porpoise but with improved equipment and a glass-fibre superstructure fore and aft of the fin in all except *Orpheus* which uses light aluminium alloy. A number of these excellent boats have been supplied to other navies: Australia (6), Brazil (3), Canada (3) and Chile (2); the remaining thirteen still serve with the Royal Navy, where their replacement is becoming a matter of some concern.

One of these submarines—*Onyx*—played a very active role in the South Atlantic War of 1982. *Onyx* landed soldiers of the Special Air Service (SAS) and marines of the Special Boat Service (SBS) on the Falkland Islands well ahead of the arrival of the main body of the task force, a mission for which the conventional submarine is still particularly suited.

Fixed-Wing Aircraft

Aircraft have been used to hunt and attack submarines since World War I, but they really came into their own in World War II. During the latter war ASW aircraft were generally either purpose-built flying-boats (e.g. Catalina, Sunderland) or converted bombers (Liberator, Lancaster). Today, however, the main type is the large converted civil airliner (Orion, Nimrod, May) although the purpose-built Atlantic is a particularly successful ASW design and just two types of flying boat remain (but are unlikely to be replaced). Only one fixed-wing ASW carrier-borne aircraft—the Lockheed Viking—serves in significant numbers, although a few Breguet Alizés are still in service with the French and Indian Navies.

Fixed-wing ASW aircraft offer long range, extended time on station and a good payload, devoted to both weapons and sensors. Their principal sensor is the sonobuoy, and they sow 'fields' which they can deploy rapidly and then monitor for hours at a time. They also carry a magnetic anomaly detector (MAD), with the magnetometer on a boom, fixed in most cases, but extendible in the case of the smaller Viking. Weapons

include torpedoes, depth charges and depth bombs (which may be nuclear).

Well over 500 Lockheed P-3 Orions are in service around the world, and the type is being updated regularly; no successor airframe is being discussed at the moment. The corresponding Soviet aircraft is the Il-38 May, which is similar in most respects to the Orion. The Atlantic has sold well in Europe and is clearly an effective machine; it is, however, one of the few twin-engined, land-based ASW aircraft, most of the others being four-engined. One that stands apart is the British Nimrod, which is turbojet (as opposed to turboprop) powered. The argument for this is that it enables the aircraft to reach the scene of its patrol more rapidly, although the fact that the Comet was the only British airframe available at the time may have had something to do with its selection.

Below: The first BAe Nimrod MR Mk 2 for the Royal Air Force. Fixed-wing ASW aircraft provide an extremely cost-effective ASW platform, especially when operating in conjunction with sea-bed sensors. They can cover vast areas and carry a useful payload.

Dassault-Breguet Atlantic

(France)

Type: Long-range maritime patrol aircraft (crew of 12).
Dimensions: Length 107ft (32·62m); span 122·4ft (37·3m); height 37·25ft (11·35m).
Weight: Empty 55,775lb (25,300kg); maximum 101,850lb (46,200kg).
Engines: Two 6,220ehp Rolls-Royce Tyne 21 two-shaft turboprops.
Performance: Maximum speed 355kt (658km/h) at altitude; patrol speed 170kt (315km/h); service ceiling 30,000ft (9,150m); patrol endurance 18hr; ferry range 4,400nm (8,150km).
Payload: Weapons bay for 8 homing torpedoes or 2 AM.39 air-to-surface missiles, depth charges and bombs; 4 underwing racks for up to 7,716lb (3,500kg) of stores including rockets, air-to-surface missiles or containers.

Most land-based ASW aircraft have been produced by converting existing designs, nowadays usually airliners. The Dassault-Breguet Atlantic was, however, specially designed for the ASW task, and a total of 87 was produced for the naval air forces of France, Germany, Italy and the Netherlands between 1964 and 1974. The type thus came very close to being the standard West European maritime patrol aircraft; indeed, it nearly succeeded in attracting an order from the Royal Air Force. The only export order—three machines for Pakistan—was met by selling three of the French Aéronavale machines.

By the mid-1970s a requirement for a follow-on design to replace both the Atlantic and the few remaining Lockheed P-2 Neptunes was identified, and it was decided that this could best be met by a new version of the Breguet aircraft. Design studies in 1977–78 led to the Atlantic Nouvelle Génération (NG). Changes to the airframe are limited to improvements in sealing, bonding and anti-corrosion, particularly to the elevator control system, failure of which was alleged to have caused several of the original aircraft to crash.

The major changes are in the avionics and the chin turret of the SAT/TRT FLIR (forward-looking infra-red) sensor makes the new aircraft instantly recognisable. Atlantic NG carries a Thomson-CSF Iguane I-band radar with a retractable ventral radome containing an integrated radar/IFF antenna and offering track-while-scan performance on up to 100 targets simultaneously. Antennas in the wing tips and in a fin-mounted pod feed the ARAR-13 ESM equipment, a passive receiver believed to cover the radar spectrum from 2·5 to 18·0GHz.

The prominent tail 'sting' houses a Crouzet MAD sensor which incorporates two detector elements whose outputs are compared in order to measure the residual magnetic field of the aircraft, providing automatic compensation for changes due to different stores loads. All systems in the avionics installations are linked to a digital data bus, whilst a Thomson-CSF Cimesa digital computer processes and collates the tactical data from the sensors ready for display to the crew.

Armament carried in the weapons bay includes homing torpedoes, depth charges or AM.39 Exocet ASMs. A smaller bay further aft carries up to 78 sonobuoys, usually a mixture of TSM 8010 and the newer, lighter and more capable TSM 8020.

Dassault-Breguet converted two existing Atlantic airframes as prototype Atlantic NGs, the first flying on 8 May 1981. The Aéronavale requires 42 aircraft, and deliveries are due to start in 1986. Construction will be carried out by the same international consortium that built the original aircraft, i.e. Aérospatiale and Dassault-Breguet (France), Dornier and MBB (West Germany), Aeritalia (Italy) and Fokker, SABCA and Sonaca (Netherlands). No other orders for the Atlantic NG have been announced, although West Germany plans to update its present fleet, a $44 million contract having been given to Loval for unspecified work.

**Above: Dassault-Breguet Atlantic Nouvelle Génération (NG),
showing its characteristic chin turret and revised topline to the
fin. 42 of these aircraft have been ordered by the French Navy
with deliveries commencing in 1986, but whether export orders
will be forthcoming remains to be seen.**

**Below: Italian Air Force Atlantic Br.1150 flies over a surfaced
submarine; 18 were built in Italy by Aeritalia.**

Shin Meiwa PS-1

(Japan)

Type: ASW flying boat (crew of 9).
Dimensions: Fuselage length 109·9ft (33·5m); span 108·7ft (33·14m); height 31·9ft (9·7m).
Weight: Empty 58,000lb (26,300kg); maximum 94,800lb (43,000kg).
Engines: Four 3,060ehp Ishikawajima-built General Electric T64-IHI-10 single-shaft turboprops.
Performance: Maximum speed 295kt (547km/h); service ceiling 29,500ft (9,000m); range (loaded) 1,170nm (2,167km).
Payload: 4 depth bombs; 4 Mk 44/46 homing torpedoes; launchers on wing tips for triple groups of 5in rockets.

The 1966 JASDF decision to proceed with the development of a new ASW flying boat was a brave one, and was based on the theory that a flying boat is a near ideal ASW platform because it can alight on the water to conduct sonar searches. This not only gives a more effective sonar capability, but also saves on the not inconsiderable cost of sonobuoys. In practice, however, the land-based ASW aircraft have proved a more cost-effective solution

and the Soviet Beriev Be-12 and the Shin Meiwa PS-1 are unlikely to be followed by further flying boats.

The first of two PS-1 prototypes flew on 5 October 1967, and both were extensively tested, especially for seaworthiness. Due to spiralling costs only 23 PS-1s were built, of which 19 survive in 1984. The PS-1 can operate in wave heights up to 14 ft (4·3m), allowing operations in the Pacific for 80 per cent of the time. A compressor mounted in the upper fuselage provides air for boundary-layer control, and this, combined with blown trailing-edge flaps, gives a take-off speed of less than 50kt (90km/h), remarkable for such a large aircraft.

The crew consists of two pilots, a navigator, an engineer, a radio operator, a MAD operator, two sonar operators and a tactical co-ordinator. Sono-buoys, smoke bombs and depth charges are carried in an internal weapons bay, whilst underwing pods each contain two homing torpedoes and launchers for unguided rockets can be fitted to the wingtips. A tricycle undercarriage is fitted for use when beaching.

Below: Shin Meiwa US-1 amphiblan search-and-rescue aircraft (foreground) is essentially similar to the PS-1 ASW aircraft (behind). Intended to alight on the surface to conduct sonar searches, this is one of two remaining flying-boat types.

Kawasaki P-2J

(Japan)

Type: Land-based LRMP aircraft.
Dimensions: Length 95·9ft (29·32m); span 101·3ft (30·87m); height 29·3ft (8·93m).
Weight: Empty 42,500lb (19,277kg); maximum 75,000lb (34,019kg).
Engines: Two 2,850hp General Electric T64-10 single-shaft turboprops; two 3,085lb (1,400kg) thrust Ishikawajima-Harima J3-7C turbojets.
Performance: Maximum speed (jets) 350kt (649km/h); typical cruising speed 217kt (402km/h); service ceiling 30,000ft (9,144m); range 2,400nm (4,445km).
Payload: Mk 44/46 homing torpedoes, depth bombs, rockets; maximum internal load 8,000lb (3,630kg).

The Kawasaki P-2J was based upon the P-2H (a Japanese adaptation of the Lockheed P-2) which preceded it in JMSDF service. Design began in 1961, but the first production aircraft did not fly until August 1969 and the last of 89 was not delivered until 10 years later. The whole programme appears, with the benefit of hindsight, to have been a mistake, possibly because it was ten years too late.

Although the JMSDF was at pains to procure a much more capable aircraft than the P-2H, some of the changes did little to enhance operational effectiveness. Replacing the piston-engines by turboprops, for example, saved weight, but was offset by the greater fuel consumption. The twin-wheel main landing gear is, however, better than the previous large single wheels, and the much longer fuselage allows a crew of 12 to operate in reasonable comfort. A comprehensive suite of navigation and attack sensors is fitted, but this has had to be updated in the course of the lengthy production run. ASW sensors include the Julie/Jezebel acoustic system, ARR-52A(V) sonobuoy receiver and HSQ-101MAD installation. The original search radar was the APS-80(J), but this was replaced by the APS-80(N) in later aircraft, although even this is now out of date.

By 1981 the P-2J force was beginning to be reduced by converting aircraft for other purposes. Replacement by the much more capable P-3C/Update II will take place over the years 1982-88.

Below: Kawasaki P-2J, a Japanese development of the Neptune.

Beriev Be-12 (M-12) Mail

(Soviet Union)

Type: Multi-role reconnaissance amphibian (crew of 4–9).
Dimensions: Length 99ft (30·17m); span 97·5ft (29·71m); height 23ft (7m).
Weight: Empty 44,092lb (20,000kg); maximum 64,925lb (29,450kg).
Engines: Two 4,190ehp Ivchenko AI-20D single-shaft turboprops.
Performance: Maximum speed 329kt (610km/h); service ceiling 37,000ft (11,280m); range 2,160nm (4,000km); operational radius 702nm (1,300km).
Payload: Internal weapons bay for variety of ASW weapons; 2–4 underwing hardpoints for homing torpedoes or other stores.

Only two types of the once numerous ASW amphibians remain in service—the Soviet Beriev Be-12 and the Japanese Shin Meiwa PS-1—and even these are now gradually being phased out. The Beriev design bureau has produced a series of amphibious aircraft for the Soviet Naval Air Force over the years, but the M-12 Tchaika will almost certainly prove to have been the last of the line. Total production was of the order of 100 aircraft, all of which served with either the Black Sea or the Northern Fleet. None have been exported, and some seen over the Mediterranean in the 1960s in Egyptian markings were later discovered to have been Soviet Navy aircraft on detachment. Some eighty remain in service but, with the land-based Ilyushin Il-38 taking over the ASW role, most Be-12s have probably been relegated to second-line duties. Some ASW versions may, however, remain in service, perhaps with updated systems, for use in tactical situations where the ability to alight on water and conduct a sonar search may be of value.

The weapons bay is situated in the rear section of the fuselage, and there are two stores pylons under each wing; hatches in the rear fuselage permit weapons to be loaded while the aircraft is moored afloat. At least 6,500lb (3,000kg) of stores can be carried, and during a record-breaking flight in 1974 a Be-12 flew around a closed-circuit course carrying an 11,075lb (5,023kg) payload. Homing torpedoes, depth charges and sonobuoys are stored in the weapons bay, and air-to-surface missiles, unguided rockets and free-fall bombs are carried on the underwing pylons.

Below: Beriev Be-12, an ASW amphibian, is now being phased out.

Ilyushin Il-38

(Soviet Union)

Type: LRMP aircraft (crew of 8–12).
Dimensions: Length 129·8ft (39·6m); span 122·7ft (37·4m); height 35ft (10·7m).
Weight: Empty 80,470lb (36,500kg); maximum 143,300lb (65,000kg).
Engines: Four 4,250ehp Ivchenko AI-20M single-shaft turboprops.
Performance: Maximum speed 380kt (704km/h) at altitude; patrol speed 174kt (322km/h); range 3,900nm (7,223km); patrol endurance 12hr.
Payload: Weapons bay for homing torpedoes, depth bombs, sonobuoys; maximum total load 15,432lb (7,000kg).

Like the US Navy's P-3 Orion, the Ilyushin Il-38 (May) was developed from a turboprop passenger transport, in this case the Il-18 Coot. It is a new and purpose-built variant designed to incorporate the necessary sensors and weapons for ASW search and strike. Modifications to the basic Il-18 design include moving the wing forward to counter a shift in the centre of gravity caused by the weapons bay. A prominent search radar is fitted beneath the forward fuselage; the rear fuselage contains only sensors (including a MAD stinger in the tail) and sonobuoy launchers. The fuselage has the same

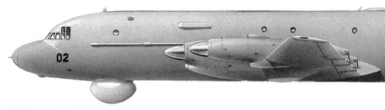

cross-section as that of the civil transport; the weapons bay, and consequently the payload, is thus small by Western standards, although there are four hardpoints under the wings for external stores. External inspection suggests an austere electronics fit, but Soviet capabilities in this area should never be underestimated. There is a flight crew of four and a tactical crew of eight who are almost certainly assisted by an on-board computer. Offensive payload includes gravity bombs, depth charges, ASW torpedoes and nuclear depth bombs.

Some seventy aircraft of this type are in service with the AV-MF, and a small number have been supplied to the Indian Navy. Some Il-38s operated from Egyptian bases in the early 1970s in support of Soviet ASW operations in the eastern Mediterranean, and others deploy overseas from time to time. The most likely mission for the Il-38 in the event of war between NATO and the Warsaw Pact is direct support of the Soviet Navy's own ballistic missile submarines (SSBNs) in the Northern and Pacific fleet areas.

Below: Ilyushin Il-38 long-range maritime patrol aircraft of the Indian Navy; six are in current service.

Below: A Soviet Navy Il-38 May on patrol.

Tupolev Tu-20 Bear

(Soviet Union)

Type: Long-range ASW patrol aircraft (crew of 7–12).

Dimensions: Length 162·4ft (49·5m); span 167·7ft (51·1m); height 39·75ft (12·12m).

Weight: Empty 178,571lb (81,000kg); maximum 414,462lb (188,000kg).

Engines: Four 14,795ehp Kuznetsov NK-12M turboprops.

Performance: Maximum speed 456kt (845km/h) at altitude; cruise speed 378kt (700km/h); service ceiling 44,300ft (13,500m); range 6,775nm (12,550km); patrol endurance 28hr.

Payload: 6 23mm cannon in three remotely-controlled barbettes; homing torpedoes, depth bombs, sonobuoys in internal bomb-bay.

In creating this intercontinental bomber, Tupolev selected the unlikely combination of turboprop propulsion and a swept wing, a formula rejected by the West, although the Tu-95/142 series seems to have been none the less effective for that! Early types had a top speed of 510kt (950km/h), although this speed could not be matched by current service aircraft, which have a top speed of no more than 470kt (870km/h) at best. Normal cruising is around 405kt (750km/h).

Below: Latest version of the Bear is the -F, a specialised long-range maritime patrol aircraft with many new sensors.

Some 100 Tu-95s still serve as bombers with the Long-Range Aviation component of the Soviet Air Force, and a further 70 Bears are used by Soviet Naval Aviation for maritime reconnaissance, a task for which the type's long range makes it well suited. These aircraft have been given a separate designation by the Soviet Union as Tu-142. The first sub-type was Bear-C, a simple adaptation of Bear-B. The main task of the later Bear-D is thought to be over-the-horizon targeting for anti-ship missiles (e.g. SS-N-3, SS-N-12). Bear-E is an Elint variant with an array of camera ports in the weapons bay.

Many aircraft are now being upgraded to Bear-F standard, this type now comprising about half of the Soviet Navy's Bear fleet. It features extended nacelles on the inboard engines (probably to reduce drag), an extended front fuselage, a repositioned ventral radome and additional stowage bays in the rear fuselage. Bulged nosewheel doors suggest a reconfigured under-carriage, perhaps to make the aircraft more suitable for use from poor runways.

The latest sub-type is dubbed Bear-G by NATO and features a stretched front fuselage, and it is believed that the new section houses additional ASW electronic equipment. The total Bear-F/G fleet is believed to number some fifty aircraft, divided between two independent ASW regiments serving the Northern and Pacific Fleets and a training unit at the Soviet Navy's flying school near Moscow. It is suggested in some quarters that a new long-range Soviet ASW aircraft is under development, and this would seem logical as the Bear airfames must be approaching the end of their useful lives.

BAe (HSA) Nimrod

(UK)

Type: LRMP aircraft (crew of 12).
Dimensions: Length 126·75ft (38·63m); span 114·8ft (35m); height 29·7ft (9·1m).
Weight: Empty 92,000lb (41,730kg); maximum 192,000lb (87,090kg).
Engines: Four 12,140lb (5,507kg) thrust Rolls-Royce Spey 250 two-shaft turbofans.
Performance: Maximum speed 500kt (926km/h); patrol speed 425kt (787km/h); service ceiling 42,000ft (12,800m); range 5,000nm (9,260km); patrol endurance 12hr.
Payload: Internal weapons bay for up to 6 Mk 46/Stingray homing torpedoes, depth bombs, sonobuoys; 2 wing pylons for Martel or AS.12 ASMs (some MR.2s fitted for AIM-9 Sidewinder AAMs).

Right: An RAF Nimrod MR.1 circles over a surfaced Soviet submarine in the North Atlantic, rehearsing a war situation.

Below: Victor K.2 tanker refuelling a Nimrod MR.2. During the South Atlantic War the British discovered that air-to-air refuelling is essential for every type of military aircraft to meet unexpected contingencies—a lesson never to be forgotten?

Like many other LRMP aircraft, the Nimrod is adapted from a civil airliner but, quite unlike any other in this role, it is powered by gas turbines instead of turboprops. The Nimrod was derived from the De Havilland Comet 4, the direct descendant of the world's first jet airliner. A major advantage of jet propulsion is that the Nimrod has a high transit speed, and can thus react quickly to a submarine datum established by a broad-area detection system such as SOSUS or by passive arrays towed by ships.

Forty-nine aircraft were built; of these, forty-three were to the MR.1 (ASW) standard, three were completed as R.1 Elint aircraft, and three were diverted from MR.1 to become trials aircraft for the AEW.3 programme. The original MR.1 was reliable, but its effectiveness in the ASW role was inhibited by its relatively austere avionics fit. This is being overcome by a major modernisation programme involving the installation of the EMI Searchwater radar, a Marconi AQS-901 acoustic processing and display system matched to the Barra sonobuoy, and a new Central Tactical Data system based on a Marconi 920 ATC digital computer. Thirty-four MR.1s are being converted to this MR.2 standard, whilst the remainder of the Nimrod force will be converted to AEW.3s to replace the desperately ageing Shackletons. The ASW Nimrods serve with four RAF squadrons: No 42 at St Mawgan, and Nos 120, 201 and 206 at Kinloss.

Grumman S-2 Tracker

(USA)

Type: Carrier/land-based ASW and patrol aircraft (crew of 4).
Dimensions: Length 43·5ft (13·26m); span 72·6ft (22·13m); height 16·6ft (5·06m).
Weight: Empty 18,750lb (8,505kg); maximum 29,150lb (13,222kg).
Engines: Two 1,525hp Wright R-1820-82WA Cyclone nine-cylinder radials.
Performance: Maximum speed 230kt (426km/h) at sea level; service ceiling 21,000ft (6,400m); range 1,130nm (2,095km).
Payload: 2 homing torpedoes, 2 Mk 101 depth bombs or 4 385lb (175kg) depth charges in internal weapons bay; 6 underwing pylons for bombs or rockets.

First flown on 4 December 1952 as the S2F-1, the Tracker was the first effective hunter/killer ASW platform for operation against modern submarines from carriers of the US Navy. Its twin Wright Cyclone engines enabled it to carry both sensors and weapons, combining the missions which had previously required a team of two aircraft, one a hunter and the other a killer; further, its piston engines and long-span wings enabled it to operate safely from small ASW carriers, thus freeing the larger attack

carriers for other aircraft types. This automatically enabled the Tracker to use even the poorest military airfields in some of the countries where it has subsequently served.

There have been many versions, with progressively updated equipment. The main type in use today is the S-2E, the best of the ASW variants, although a few of the earlier versions, notably the original S-2A, can still be found. All S-2 variants have a basic crew of four. The pilot sits on the left and the co-pilot on the right doing most of the navigating; the two radar operators sit in the rear seats, handling both the radar and other sensors such as a retractable MAD boom in the rear fuselage, sixty echo-sounding charges dropped in sequence as part of the Julie active system and AQA-3 Jezebel passive long-range acoustic search equipment. The rear of each engine nacelle houses sixteen sonobuoys, and a searchlight is normally fitted outboard of the starboard engine. An ALD-3 direction-finding (DF) set is carried to pinpoint submarine radio transmissions, its antenna housed prominently above the cockpit. The S-2 also has some capability against surface ships.

In the South Atlantic War of 1982, the six old S-2As of the Argentine Navy did not see action, but against a less sophisticated enemy in a limited war they could play a useful role against conventional submarines. At a modest cost the S-2 combines fair performance with an endurance of some nine hours, even when carrying several tons of obsolescent avionics.

Left: An early model Grumman S-2 Tracker of the US Navy with its Magnetic Anomaly Detector (MAD) boom extended. Because it was designed to use small carriers, the S-2 has an excellent take-off capability, which has made it popular with smaller air forces wanting a cheap ASW aircraft.

Below: S-2F Tracker of the Dutch Navy. The main search radar antenna is in the retractable ventral bin, and in this view the MAD boom is still housed in the rear fuselage. There are 16 sonobuoys in the rear of each engine nacelle. Although no longer in service with major navies a number still serve in the Third World.

S-2A-169

KON.MARINE

Lockheed S-3 Viking

(USA)

Type: Carrier-based ASW aircraft (crew of 4).

Dimensions: Length 53·3ft (16·26m); span 68·7ft (20·93m); height 22·75ft (6·93m).

Weight: Empty 26,783lb (12,149kg); maximum 52,539lb (23,832kg).

Engines: Two 9,275lb (4,207kg) thrust General Electric TF34-400 two-shaft turbofans.

Performance: Maximum speed 440kt (814km/h) at sea level; service ceiling 35,000ft (10,670m); ferry range 3,000nm (5,556km); mission range 2,000nm (3,705km); mission endurance 9hr.

Payload: 2/4 Mk 46 homing torpedoes; 2/4 depth bombs in internal weapons bays; 2 wing pylons for Harpoon missiles, bombs, rockets or fuel tanks.

Designed to replace the Grumman S-2 Tracker (qv) in the carrier-borne fixed-wing role for the US Navy, the Lockheed S-3 Viking is a very sophisticated aircraft equipped with the most advanced detection and data processing capabilities. Sensors include a high resolution radar (APS-116) for maritime reconnaissance, MAD (ASQ-81(V)), FLIR, and sixty sonobuoys for submarine detection. Behind the pilot and co-pilot sit the Tactical Coordinator (TACCO) and the Sensor Operator (SENSO). The primary data display is the ASA-82 system, which serves as a real-time link between the four-man crew and the various surface and underwater sensors. Information is stored, updated, refreshed and selectively displayed by the AYK-30 on-board digital computer.

Below: S-3A Viking of US Navy squadron VS-41, a shore-based training unit. All US Navy aircraft carriers except *Midway* and *Coral Sea* now operate ten of these aircraft for long-range ASW patrol. They are particularly necessary to deal with the threat from Soviet Navy cruise-missile submarines, which are specifically intended to attack US Navy carrier groups.

Above: Two USN S-3A Vikings set off on patrol; they belong to squadron VS-22, serving aboard the carrier _Saratoga_. They are carrying gravity bombs on the underwing pylons, which, in the S-3B version, will also be able to take the Harpoon anti-ship missile. Numerous antennas can be seen, as can the tip of the retracted MAD boom, beneath the horizontal stabiliser.

The initial production order of 184 aircraft was completed by FY77. From the mid-1970s, fixed-wing squadrons, each of ten S-3A Vikings, were added to the air groups of all the US Navy's multi-purpose aircraft carriers (CV), except for the two older ships of the Midway class. There was some initial criticism of the additional maintenance load imposed by the S-3A, but its ability to react quickly and effectively to a distant underwater contact has proved invaluable.

A contract has recently been signed for the upgrading of 160 aircraft to S-3B standard, which involves an increase in acoustic and radar processing capabilities, expanded electronic support measures (ESM), a new sonobuoy receiver system (ARR-78(V)) and the Harpoon anti-ship missile. This last will, of course, add considerably to the carriers' already strong attack potential.

Below: An excellent tail view of an S-3A on the ground, showing the tip of the retracted MAD boom in the tail. Underneath, the chutes for the sonobuoys are visible, as are the underwing pylons for external loads.

Lockheed P-3 Orion

(USA)

Type: LRMP aircraft (crew of ten).
Dimensions: Length 116·8ft (35·61m); span 99·7ft (30·37m); height 33·7ft (10·29m).
Weight: Empty 61,491lb (27,890kg); maximum 142,000lb (64,410kg).
Engines: Four 4,910shp Allison T56-14 single-shaft turboprops.
Performance: Maximum speed 410kt (761km/h); service ceiling 28,300ft (8,625m); range 4,500nm (8,334km); patrol endurance 16hr.
Payload: Weapons bay for 4 Mk 46 torpedoes, depth bombs, sonobuoys; 4 wing pylons each rated at 2,000lb (907kg) for Mk 46 torpedoes or Harpoon ASMs.

Above: P-3C of the US Navy on patrol over coastal waters. The original Lockheed Electra was one of the more unsuccessful airliners, but the P-3 Orion is a very big success, with over 500 delivered.

Right: P-3C Update II photographed in 1977. Note the infrared detector in the small chin turret and the wing-tip pylons for Harpoon missiles. The long tail boom for the MAD detector is also very evident, as are the launch tubes for sonobuoys located in the fuselage belly.

A 1957 US Navy requirement for an 'off the shelf' LRMP aircraft based on an existing airframe to replace the ageing P-2 Neptune was met by Lockheed's proposed conversion of the Electra airliner, the P-3A Orion. The airframe was shortened by 12ft (3·65m), strengthened, equipped for weapons delivery and given increased fuel capacity. The avionics were initially those of the P-2, but improvements were made during the P-3A production run, with yet more in the P-3B (which also had more powerful engines).

The P-3C entered service in 1969, displaying few differences externally but with significant advances in ASW capability. Acoustic operators in earlier aircraft tended to be overwhelmed by the quantity of sensor data, much of which was unusable, and to be handicapped by inadequate time in which to make decisions. This was resolved by introducing digital computers to record and analyse sensor data. As a result, acoustic operators in the P-3C monitor sixteen sonobuoys compared to eight in the P-3B and only four in the P-3A. The nine-sonobuoy launch chutes of the P-3A/B were increased to 48 externally-loaded chutes, plus one reloadable internal tube; low-light television (LLTV) replaced the searchlights; a FLIR dome replaced the chin gondola for cameras; improvements were made in passive electronic counter-measures (ECM), and installation of the AQS-81 MAD (from the 43rd P-3C) doubled detection range. A computer cross-references all these sensors and automatically relates data to position information from an improved navigation system.

The formidable capabilities of the P-3C are being further enhanced by a series of 'update' programmes. Update I (in service 1974) included the Omega navigation system, a new tactical display and a six-fold increase in computer memory. Update II (1978) included an improved acoustic recording system, provision for firing the Harpoon ASM, FLIR in place of LLTV, and a sonobuoy reference system similar to that of the S-3 Viking. The P-3C Update III is now entering service. The major change is the installation of the IBM UYS-1 acoustic signal processor, which has taken some time to get right as it affects virtually every other element of the aircraft's systems. At this rate the P-3 can be expected to serve well into the 21st Century. ▶

The Electra was something of a failure as an airliner: only 170 were built, well short of the break-even figure. The Orion, however, has been an outstanding success, and deliveries now total well over 500, with production still in full swing. The US Navy operates 24 active squadrons of nine P-3Cs each, plus 13 Naval Reserve squadrons with P-3A/Bs. P-3Bs are operated by New Zealand (5) and Norway (7); P-3Cs are operated by Australia (20), and the Netherlands has 13 on order. Iran received six P-3Fs in the Shah's time, but only one or two are now serviceable. Japan is building 42 P-3Cs under licence in addition to three delivered direct from Lockheed, whilst Canada has replaced her fleet of 26 CP-121 Arguses with 18 new CP-140 Auroras, a variant of the P-3C built to Canadian specifications and incorporating the complete sensor and processing systems of the S-3A Viking.

Right: Loading a sonobuoy into the chute of a P-3 Orion. The sonobuoy is a very effective sensor, but it is not recoverable and therefore works out too expensive for many navies.

Below: A fine overhead shot of a US Navy P-3 Orion, with a particularly good view of the MAD tail 'stinger'. MAD is an extremely sensitive device, but is only used when other sensors have first detected a submarine's presence. Other versions of the P-3 are for weather reconnaissance and Elint work.

ASW Helicopters

Almost from the machine's inception, the possibility of using the helicopter at sea was in the minds of designers and naval staffs alike. The US Navy was using Sikorsky R-4s at sea in 1943, but for the next ten years or so their role was limited to reconnaissance and liaison. Gradually, however, the potential of the helicopter as an ASW platform began to be realised. The US Navy went off at a tangent for some years with DASH, a radio-controlled drone helicopter carrying a torpedo, but it was the Royal Canadian Navy which pioneered the use of manned helicopters from a flight deck on the sterns of destroyers and frigates—a practice which is now almost universal. Initially, these simply carried torpedoes to the area dictated by the parent ship's sensors, but as sensors and processors have become smaller and lighter, ASW helicopters have become increasingly autonomous. Today's larger ASW helicopters, such as the SH-3 Sea King and Lynx, are highly capable ASW systems in their own right. Indeed, so capable are these types that a new type of ship has been created—the helicopter carrier—whose sole reason for existence is to act as a platform for these very effective sub-hunters.

Helicopters hunt submarines using either dunking sonar or sonobuoys. Dunking sonar is an effective short-range system, although the active systems are

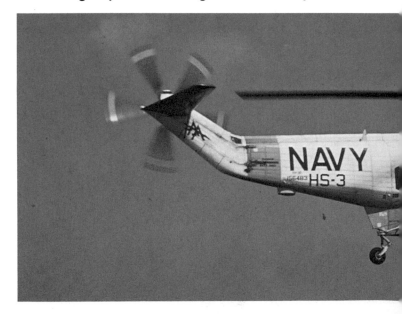

limited in performance by the size of the helicopter carrying them. The major shortcoming is that the helicopter must hover close to the surface while 'dunking', which consumes much fuel and prevents the aircraft from being used for other roles at the same time. Sonobuoys are more effective and release the helicopter from the hovering problem, but because they are expendable they become very expensive—the last admitted US annual expenditure on sonobuoys was $74 million, a price well beyond the reach of most navies. Helicopters also employ MAD, a useful passive system for confirming a target's presence. They usually deploy the magnetometer in a 'bird' towed behind the aircraft on a cable, although a Canadian company is now offering a built-in design for helicopters.

The primary ASW weapon for helicopters is the torpedo, which can be dropped very close to the target. Depth charges can also be carried, and some sources suggest that nuclear depth bombs are carried by certain nations' ASW helicopters.

Below: An SH-3 ASW helicopter taking off from the deck of USS *Forrestal*. In the past decade the helicopter has progressed from merely an extension of the ship's sensors to an autonomous and extremely effective weapons system in its own right.

Aérospatiale Super Frelon

(France)

Type: Shipborne/land-based ASW helicopter (crew of 5).
Dimensions: Fuselage length 63·6ft (19·4m); main rotor diameter 62ft (18·9m); height 16·2ft (4·9m).
Weight: Empty 15,130lb (6,863kg); maximum 28,660lb (13,000kg).
Engines: Three 1,570shp Turboméca Turmo IIIC$_6$ turboshafts.
Performance: Maximum speed 148kt (275km/h); service ceiling 10,325ft (3,150m); range 440nm (815km); mission endurance 4hr.
Payload: 4 Mk 44/46 homing torpedoes or 2 AM.39 ASMs.

The Aérospatiale 321 Super Frelon is the largest helicopter to be designed and built in Western Europe. Production began in 1965 and still continues; to date, 99 have been ordered. It was derived from Aérospatiale's SA 3200 Frelon but incorporates technology 'bought in' from other companies: the main lift and tail rotors and their drive systems were designed with assistance from Sikorsky, who also helped with the boat-shaped hull; and Fiat assisted with the main gearbox and power transmission. The Super Frelon is built in two main variants, the SA 321G all-weather ASW model and the SA 321Ja transport version.

Twenty-four Super Frelon SA 321Gs were built for the Aéronavale: ten serve with squadron 32F in the ASW role and the remainder as transport helicopters with 27F and 33F. A number of SA 321Gs of 32F have operated from the carriers *Clémenceau* and *Foch* in recent years, and 32F is also responsible for ASW operations in support of France's ballistic missile submarines (SNLE). These duties include 'de-lousing' the SNLEs as they leave port to start their patrols. The SA 321Gs generally operate in groups of up to four aircraft, with one employing its Sylphe panoramic dunking sonar for listening while the others make their attacks. Equipment includes a 360° search radar, doppler navigation radar, dunking sonar and up to four homing torpedoes. French Navy aircraft are being updated, the Héraclès ORB radar being replaced by the more powerful Héraclès II version which doubles the range and also is compatible with the AM.39 Exocet anti-ship missile.

The Libyan Air Force operates nine SA 321Ms in the ASW/SAR roles. Iraq operates ten Super Frelons armed with Exocet in the ship attack role, and has a further three on order. The People's Republic of China has purchased thirteen Super Frelons for naval use, but (so far as is known) only in the transport role.

Above: A Super Frelon of the French Aéronavale with its dunking sonar deployed. These aircraft are having their systems upgraded, but the whole fleet will need replacing by about 1990.

Above: An SA 321G just after lifting its Sylphe panoramic
dunking sonar from the sea. Note also the large nose-mounted
Héraclès search radar. An SAR version is also in service.

Agusta-Bell AB 212

(Italy/USA)

Type: Shipborne ASW helicopter (crew of 3–4).
Dimensions: Fuselage length 45·9ft (14m); main rotor diameter 48ft (14·6m); height 12·8ft (3·9m).
Weight: Empty 7,540lb (3,420kg); maximum 11,200lb (5,080kg).
Engines: One 1,875shp United Aircraft of Canada PT6T-3 Turbo Twin Pac.
Performance: Maximum speed 106kt (196km/h); service ceiling 14,200ft (4,330m); range 315nm (584km); mission endurance 3hr.
Payload: 2 Mk 44/46 homing torpedoes or 4 AS.12 ASMs.

Agusta-Bell developed the AB 204 from the basic Bell UH-1 utility helicopter for use by the Regia Aeronautica. An ASW variant—AB 204AS—was also developed, for use from a series of anti-submarine cruisers and frigates built for the Italian Navy during the 1960s. These aircraft work in pairs, one being fitted with an AQS-13B dunking sonar and the other with two Mk 44/46 homing torpedoes. The AB 204AS is unusual among shipborne helicopters in that it utilises a skid undercarriage instead of the more generally used castored wheels. Some two dozen AB 204ASs remain in service but are being progressively replaced by the newer and much more capable AB 212.

Right: Agusta developed the AB 204 from the basic UH-1 and the ASW version is the AB 204AS. The aircraft seen here is on board the Italian Bergamini class frigate _Carlo Margottini_. The days of the 204 in Italian Navy service are now numbered.

Below: The AB 212AS is a great advance on the AB 204, and almost one hundred are on order. A powerful search radar is fitted above the cabin, and both sonobuoys and dunking sonar are carried. Retention of skids is unique in ASW helicopters.

The AB 212 is similar in overall dimensions to its predecessor but represents a great increase in capability, not the least being that it can operate in the ASW role autonomously, whereas the earlier type could only operate as part of a team of two. A more powerful search radar is fitted in a prominent radome on the cabin roof, and sonobuoys are carried in addition to the AQS-13B dunking sonar. Four AS.12 missiles can be carried for the surface attack role, and the TG-2 system enables the AB 212AS to provide mid-course guidance for ship-launched Otomat SSMs. Like its Italian predecessor, the AB 212AS retains its skid undercarriage, with inflatable pontoons for use in an emergency landing on water.

This design is unique to Agusta-Bell, and there is no equivalent in the range offered by the parent company in the USA. Forty-eight aircraft are on order for the Italian Navy, with further machines ordered by Greece, Iraq, Peru, Turkey and Venezuela. Peru and Venezuela will operate the AB 212AS from Italian-built frigates of the Lupo class, while the Greeks will operate theirs from Dutch-built Kortenaer class frigates.

Kamov Ka-25 Hormone

(Soviet Union)

Type: Shipborne ASW helicopter (crew of 2).
Dimensions: Fuselage length 34ft (10·4m); main rotor diameter 51·7ft
(15·75m); height 17·7ft (5·4m).
Weight: Empty 10,500lb (4,765kg); maximum 16,500lb (7,500kg).
Engines: Two 900hp Glushenkov GTD-3 free-turbine turboshafts.
Performance: Maximum speed 113kt (209km/h); service ceiling 11,000ft
(3,350m); range 350nm (650km); mission endurance 1½–2hr.
Payload: 1–2 400mm homing torpedoes, nuclear or conventional depth
bombs in internal weapons bay; maximum total load 2,200lb (1,000kg). ▶

**Below: The romantic setting almost disguises the lethal role of
this Ka-25 Hormone ASW helicopter out on a sunset patrol.**

Left: Ka-25 Hormone-A ASW helicopter. Note prominent chin surface search radar and the nose-mounted 'Homeguide' Yagi antennas. The inverted flower-pot housing on the tail boom is assumed to be an electro-optical sensor, precise role unclear.

▶ The untidy and inelegant appearance of the Kamov Ka-25 (Hormone) tends to disguise the fact that the ingenious Kamov design bureau has produced a highly effective shipborne helicopter. The twin turbines provide a lot of power and in combination with the coaxial rotors give high lift; furthermore, the rotor configuration does away with the long tail boom and dangerous tail rotor found in most rotary-wing designs. The overall result is a competent and versatile machine. The Ka-25 is the current standard Soviet shipboard helicopter. It first flew in 1960, and some 460 have been built in a production run which lasted from 1966 to 1975; most remain in service and a few have been exported, to India, Syria and Yugoslavia.

Three versions have been identified. Hormone-A is the basic ASW version equipped with a chin-mounted search radar, a towed MAD sensor and a dunking sonar. Most examples are of this version. Additional sensors have been added during the last decade, but the type still lacks night-vision equipment and the ability to operate its sonar in all weathers. Some aircraft have a small fairing mounted immediately below the central tail fin, but unlike that on the Mi-14 Haze (qv) this cannot be assumed to be a float. A small cylindrical housing (resembling an inverted flower pot) is mounted above the tail boom of many aircraft. This has a transparent upper section and is presumably some sort of elecro-optical sensor. Hormone-A carries a crew comprising a pilot, a co-pilot and two or three systems operators.

A small weapons bay in the cabin floor carries a payload which can consist of combinations of sonobuoys, ASW torpedoes, depth charges, nuclear depth bombs or other stores. Some of the more recent aircraft also have a rectangular underfuselage weapons container, and most have stores racks on the starboard side of the fuselage. In addition, there is evidence of an upgrading programme to fit small 'fire-and-forget' missiles. Most aircraft have their four undercarriage wheels enclosed in inflatable pontoons, surmounted by the inflation bottles.

Hormone-B is an anti-ship missile aircraft, recognisable by its larger, more curved chin radome and an additional retractable ventral radome. This aircraft is used to acquire targets for the SS-N-12 long-range ASM. The final version, Hormone-C, is a utility and search-and-rescue (SAR) aircraft.

Right: A busy flight-deck scene aboard a Moskva class carrier. The two aircraft on the deck are Hormone-As, but the radome of the aircraft behind suggests that it is probably a Hormone-B, which is the electronic warfare version.

Above: Kamov Ka-25 Hormone ASW helicopter on the flight-deck of a Kanin class destroyer. The sailors appear to be doing maintenance on the nose radar, with the radome lying on the deck. This aircraft also has the inflatable pontoons on all wheels to give flotation in the event of an emergency landing. Note the complex rotor-head.

Left: This profile shows a standard Kamov Ka-25 Hormone-A but without the inflatable pontoons on the wheels. An interesting feature of this design is that the wheels can be raised vertically in flight to prevent radar echoes, which would degrade equipment performance.

Kamov Ka-27 Helix

(Soviet Union)

Type: Shipborne ASW helicopter (crew of 2?).
Dimensions: Fuselage length 37ft (11·3m); main rotor diameter 55ft (16·75m); height 18ft (5·5m).
Weight: Maximum 16,535lb (7,500kg).
Engines: Two 1,000shp Glushenkov GTD-350BM turboshafts.
Performance: Performance and payload data can be assumed to be similar to those of the Ka-25 Hormone, with improvements in avionics, increased combat radius and greater weapons and sonobuoy capacity.

The Kamov Ka-27 (Helix) continues the Kamov design bureau's successful formula for a shipborne ASW helicopter, with twin co-axial rotors which remove the need for a tail rotor mounted on a lengthy tail boom. The Ka-27 was first seen during Exercise ZAPAD-81 (West-81) in the Baltic, when two helicopters of the type (one in civilian colours) operated from the new Soviet destroyer *Udaloy*. Although its cabin is slightly larger than that of the Hormone, the Helix is clearly intended to be compatible with ships capable of operating the former. Some components seem identical to the older type, but more powerful engines are fitted, whilst the rotor blades fold in the same way but are of a slightly different form. There is a box under the tail boom for the MAD 'bird' and there are boxes either side of the cabin which are assumed to be for sonobuoys. A civil crane version (Ka-32) was shown at Minsk airport during a conference on the use of aircraft in support of the Soviet national economy. It was claimed that this crane version could lift a load of 11,000lb (4,990kg) and carry it 115 miles (185km).

It seems possible that the Helix may overcome one of the shortcomings of the Hormone and be capable of all-weather and night sonar dipping operations. It may also be able to carry two of the new 17·7in (450mm) electric-powered torpedoes. Other weapons will include depth charges and nuclear depth bombs. The ASW version has been dubbed Helix-A by NATO, and a missile-guidance and Elint version is Helix-B. There have also been reports of a utility version—Helix-C—intended to transport Soviet naval infantry in amphibious landing operations.

Left: Ka-27 Helix-A on the flight deck of the new Soviet Navy cruiser *Udaloy*. Despite the complexity of the contra-rotating blades the Kamov design bureau has managed to include the folding mechanisms to enable the Helix to use the same hangar as the Hormone. Note how the aircraft is following the track.

Below: Helix-A landing on the flight deck of *Udaloy*.

Mil Mi-14 Haze

(Soviet Union)

Type: Land-based ASW helicopter (crew of 4–5?).
Dimensions: Fuselage length 60ft (18·3m); main rotor diameter 69·9ft (21·3m); height 15·6ft (4·8m).
Weight: Empty 17,650lb (8,000kg); maximum 26,460lb (12,000kg).
Engines: Two 2,200shp Isotov TV3-117A free-turbine turboshafts.
Performance: Maximum speed 140kt (260km/h); service ceiling 14,765ft (4,500m); range 270nm (500km); mission endurance 2½hr.
Payload: Homing torpedoes, depth bombs; possibly ASMs.

The Mil Mi-14 (Haze) was first seen in the mid-1970s. Clearly designed for ASW operations, it was at first thought in the West to be intended for the larger ASW ships, but it has only been seen operating from land bases. In creating this ASW helicopter for the Soviet Navy the Mil bureau has adopted the well-proven configuration of the Mil Mi-8. The fuselage has been remodelled with a boat-hull bottom which, in conjunction with spon-sons on either side of the fuselage, gives a degree of amphibious capability. There is, however, a large radome under the nose which would be liable to serious damage during a landing on water, which suggests that the amphi-bious capability may be for emergencies rather than for routine operations. The tricycle landing-gear is similar to that of the Mi-8 except that it is retractable. The basic rotor and transmission of the Mi-8 have been retained except that the tail rotor is now on the port side of the tail boom.

The most conspicuous of the sensors is a 360° search radar, its antenna in a chin-mounted radome. A towed MAD is fitted at the rear of the

Below: Mil Mi-14 Haze over Kashin class destroyer.

**Above: An airborne Haze clearly showing the mysterious
pod and box beneath the tail boom; the pod may be a float.**

fuselage. The only other evidence of sensors is a fitting beneath the tail
boom which may be a doppler radar but which is suggested by some to be a
bulky battery. A small pod-like object beneath the tail boom is a float to
prevent the rotor blades from striking the water. Sonobuoys and weapons
are carried internally.

By 1981 the Mi-14 had been deployed to all four Soviet fleets. It has also
been reported that twelve were delivered to Bulgaria in 1979. This country
is normally low on the Soviet priority list for new equipment, but in this case
there must have been a clear advantage in having another ASW helicopter
operator on the Black Sea.

Westland/Aérospatiale Lynx

(UK/France)

Type: Shipborne ASW/strike helicopter (crew of 2).
Dimensions: Fuselage length 39·6ft (12·1m); main rotor diameter 42ft (12·8m); height 11·5ft (3·5m).
Weight: Empty (basic) 6,680lb (3,030kg), (with dunking sonar) 7,370lb (3,343kg); maximum 10,500lb (4,763kg).
Engines: Two 900shp Rolls-Royce Gem 10001 or 1,120shp Gem 41-1 three-shaft turbines.
Performance: Maximum speed 145kt (269km/h); service ceiling 12,000ft (3,658m); range 320nm (593km); mission endurance (max) 2hr 50min.
Payload: (ASW) 2 Mk 46 or Stingray homing torpedoes or 2 Mk 11 depth bombs; (surface strike) 4 AS.12 or Sea Skua ASMs.

Below: Westland Lynx aboard HMS *Birmingham* (D-86).

Many modern ASW helicopters have carried out search operations against unknown, and at least sometimes potentially hostile, targets, but the Lynx is one of the very few to have actually attacked a submarine in anger: in the 1982 South Atlantic War, during the reoccupation of South Georgia, Royal Navy Lynxes caught the Argentine submarine *Sante Fé* on the surface and attacked her with wire-guided missiles and free-flight rockets, forcing her to beach and surrender.

Developed by Westland as part of the Anglo-French helicopter deal, the Lynx is built in 70/30 partnership with Aérospatiale of France. The standard version serving with the Royal Navy is the HAS.2, which is fitted with Ferranti Sea Spray search radar and a passive sonobuoy processor. Unlike the US Navy's LAMPS, the Lynx is intended to operate autonomously in the ASW role. It thus carries not only all the necessary on-board sensors (Bendix AQS-18 or Alcatel DUAV-4 'dunking sonar', ASQ-18 MAD 'bird') but also weaponry such as Mk 44 or 46 lightweight homing torpedoes or Sea Skua missiles. During the South Atlantic operations the Sea Skua missiles were launched in near-blizzard conditions, scoring five out of five hits. ▶

▶ The Lynx has sold well, and has virtually become the standard West European shipboard helicopter. The Royal Netherlands Navy has taken three successive batches: the first six (UH-14A) are for SAR, the second batch of ten (SH-14B) are HAS.2s with uprated engines and Alcatel dunking sonar, and the third batch of eight (SH-14C) are similar to the SH-14B but have MAD in place of the dunking sonar. The latter two types will operate from the frigates of the Tromp and Kortenaer classes. The twelve Mk 88 Lynxes ordered by the Federal German Navy in 1981 are for the new Bremen class frigates and are fitted with AQS-18 dunking sonar.

Above: RN Lynx: the aircraft has sold well abroad and is now virtually the standard West European shipboard ASW helicopter.

Below: Westland WG.13 Lynx of the Royal Navy carrying four anti-ship missiles, seen near RNAS, Yeovilton.

Westland Wasp

(UK)

Type: Shipborne ASW helicopter (crew of 2).
Dimensions: Fuselage length 30·3ft (9·2m); main rotor diameter 32·25ft (9·8m); height 11·7ft (3·6m).
Weight: Empty 3,452lb (1,566kg); maximum 5,500lb (2,495kg).
Engines: One derated 710shp Rolls-Royce Nimbus 503 turboshaft.
Performance: Maximum speed 104kt (193km/h); service ceiling 12,200ft (3,720m); range 263nm (488km).
Payload: 2 Mk 44/46 homing torpedoes or 2 AS.11 ASMs.

Between 1961 and 1974, Westland delivered a total of more than 250 Scout and Wasp helicopters, over 100 of which were Wasp ASW aircraft produced for the navies of Britain, Australia, Brazil, the Netherlands, New Zealand and South Africa. For shipboard use, the design had a four-element landing-gear (unlike the land-based Scout, which had skids) to enable it to straddle bulky ordnance loads such as two Mk 44 homing torpedoes. Other weaponry, including AS.11 or AS.12 wire-guided missiles, can be carried on pylons located on either side of the fuselage. Each undercarriage leg has a single castoring wheel, lockable by a sprag brake.

Although a valuable ASW weapon platform in its day, the Wasp carried no sensors, delivering homing torpedoes to the location of a hostile contact as determined by the parent vessel from sonar or via data from other aircraft or vessels. Most operated from smaller surface ships such as frigates and destroyers, as well as from auxiliary vessels such as the Royal Navy ice patrol ship *Endurance*. Most navies are now replacing their Wasps with the more powerful Lynx. The last to remain in front-line service will almost certainly be the small number serving with 22 Squadron of the South African Air Force, for which replacements will be difficult to find.

Below: Westland Wasp helicopter landing aboard the Rothesay class frigate HMS *Plymouth* (F-126).

EHI EH-101

(UK/Italy)

Type: Shipborne/land-based ASW helicopter (crew of 3–4).

Dimensions: Fuselage length 56·75ft (17·3m); main rotor diameter 60ft (18·29m); height 13·5ft (4·1m).

Weight: Empty 15,050lb (6,826kg); maximum loaded 28,660lb (13,000kg); alternative gross weight 30,000lb (13,608kg).

Engines: (Prototype) three 1,600shp General Electric T700 free-turbine turboshafts; (production) advanced T700 or three 1,917/2,500shp Rolls-Royce Turboméca RTM.321 free-turbine turboshafts.

Performance: Maximum speed (sea level) 198mph (318km/h); range (6,915kg with 3,630kg fuel) 1,265 miles (2,035km); endurance (2 engines) 9·1hr.

Payload: Homing torpedoes and ASM in internal weapons bay.

A series of British MoD(N) feasibility studies under Naval Staff Requirement 6646 (NSR.6646) were carried out in 1974–77 to define how a Sea King replacement (SKR) would operate and what sensors and performance standards it would require against the fast, deep-diving Soviet submarines anticipated in the 1990s. These showed that the best results in such an ASW role would be obtained by a helicopter having a high all-round performance, particularly long range and good endurance, and operating in the autonomous mode. The best sensors for the Atlantic Ocean and North Sea were found to be dropped sonobuoys, backed up by radar, radar intercept

equipment and MAD. As happens elsewhere, however, all these sensors would produce such a volume of data that an automated handling system would be needed. The aircraft designed to answer these requirements was designated the Westland WG.34, a machine very slightly smaller, but much more powerful than the current Sea King; it was accepted in 1978. The Italian firm Agusta decided to participate in the project in 1980, and the combined firm of Elicotteri Helicopter Industries (EHI) was formed. Aérospatiale of France has been assigned particular areas of responsibility within the project, but is not a shareholder in EHI.

In the ASW role the normal crew will be pilot, observer, acoustic systems operator and flight crewman. Equipment includes Marconi Avionics AAS-901 acoustics, Ferranti Blue Kestrel search radar (in the prominent chin-mounted radome), Decca ESM, Decca Doppler and Omega. The MAD bird will be the AQS-81 (or a later model, if available) and the data handling equipment will be by Ferranti. Comprehensive secure communications and the JTIDS digital data link will be installed.

Both Agusta and Westland will assemble the aircraft, but there will be no duplication of manufacture. A civil version is also to be produced, offering 32 seats. A market of at least 750 aircraft of all types is anticipated, with deliveries of the civil version starting in about 1988 and of the naval ASW machine in 1990.

Below: Now in full development, the EH-101 is crucial to the future of both the British and Italian helicopter industries. Westland and Agusta hope to sell this promising machine abroad as well as to their own navies; prospective market: c.750.

Kaman SH-2 Seasprite

(USA)

Type: Shipborne ASW helicopter (crew of 3).
Dimensions: Fuselage length 40·5ft (12·3m); main rotor diameter 44ft (13·4m); height 13·6ft (4·1m).
Weight: Empty 7,040lb (3,193kg); maximum 12,800lb (5,806kg).
Engines: Two 1,350shp General Electric T58-8F turboshafts.
Performance: Maximum speed 143kt (265km/h); service ceiling 22,500ft (6,858m); range (max fuel) 367nm (679km); mission endurance 2½hr.
Payload: 2 Mk 46 homing torpedoes.

Above: A Kaman SH-2F landing aboard a USN frigate. The production-line was reopened in 1981 to provide another 18 air-craft bringing the total up to some 300. Despite being labelled the 'interim' LAMPS it has given excellent service.

Charles Kaman was one of the Americans convinced of the correctness of the German Flettner intermeshing-rotor configuration, with the two axes close together but tilted outwards. Several successful designs were produced, but the SH-2 (originally designated HU2K-1) is to a more conventional formula. This exceptionally neat helicopter was initially powered by a single turbine engine mounted close under the rotor hub, and was able to carry a wide range of loads, including nine passengers and two crew. The main units of the tailwheel undercarriage retracted fully. Some 190 machines were delivered, and all were later converted to have two T58 engines in nacelles on each side of the rotor housing. All SH-2s were drastically converted in the 1970s to serve in the Light Airborne Multi-Purpose System (LAMPS) programme for anti-submarine and anti-missile defence.

The SH-2D has more than two tons of special equipment, including a powerful chin-mounted radar, sonobuoys, MAD gear, ECM, new navigation and communications systems and Mk 44 or 46 torpedoes. All these helicopters will eventually be brought up to SH-2F standard, with an improved rotor, a higher gross weight and improved sensors and weapons. Though

Above: An SH-2F about to be refuelled by its parent ship, the Knox class frigate _W S Sims_ (FF-1059). The chin radar is a Canadian Marconi LN-66HP. Note the two external fuel tanks and the red and yellow MAD 'bird', in its stowed position.

only the 'interim LAMPS' platform, the SH-2F is a substantial programme. The first of 88 new SH-2Fs became operational with HSL-33 in mid-1973 and all had been delivered by the end of the decade. Kaman then rebuilt the earlier models still in service to the new standard, and this work was completed in March 1982. Meanwhile, to meet pressing requirements, the production line was reopened in 1981 for a further run of eighteen aircraft.

Sensors fitted to the SH-2F include a Canadian Marconi LN-66HP surveillance radar with its antenna mounted in a prominent radome immediately under the nose. Other sensors are the Texas Instruments AQS-81 towed MAD and ALR-66 ESM receiver. The aircraft entered service using the SSQ-41 (passive) and SSQ-47 (active) sonobuoys, but these are being replaced by the newer Difar and Dicass models. Normal armament is a pair of homing torpedoes.

Despite its age, this helicopter still has untapped potential. As long ago as 1973 Kaman tested an SH-2F at a take-off weight 500lb (230kg) above the current limit, so payload or fuel capacity could be increased further; however, the introduction of the SH-60B (qv) is reducing its significance.

Sikorsky/Westland Sea King

(USA/UK)

Type: Shipborne/land-based ASW helicopter (crew of 4).
Dimensions: Fuselage length 54·75ft (16·7m); main rotor diameter 62ft (18·9m); height 16·8ft (5·1m).
Weight: Empty 11,865lb (5,382kg); maximum 20,500lb (9,299kg).
Engines: Two 1,400shp General Electric T58-10 turboshafts.
Performance: Maximum speed 144kt (267km/h); service ceiling 14,700ft (4,480m); range 625nm (1,160km); mission endurance 4½hr.
Payload: 2 Mk 46 homing torpedoes.
Westland-built Sea Kings have British avionics and ASW system—see text.

More than two decades after its first flight, the S-61 Sea King is still in production, more than 770 having been built by Sikorsky and a further 400-plus built under licence by Agusta (Italy), Mitsubishi (Japan), and Westland (UK). These latter are much modified from the original and are described separately below.

The S-61 started life as the HSS-2 ASW helicopter and entered service with the US Navy in the early 1960s as the SH-3A; 255 were built for the USN, with a further 41 built in Canada (as the CH-124) and 73 in Japan (as the S-61B). The next version for the US Navy was the SH-3D, powered by the T58-GE-10. This was fitted with a Bendix AQS-13 dunking sonar and could carry sonobuoys and weapons such as homing torpedoes, depth charges and depth bombs; 72 were built for the US Navy, 22 for Spain, four for Brazil and four for Argentina. This version is also built by Agusta in Italy, who have received orders for a total of 54 helicopters for the Italian Navy as well as seven for Iran. Some of the Agusta-built SH-3Ds have been fitted with a Sistel APQ-706 search radar and armed with Martel SSMs.

The current SH-3H has new ASW equipment and all remaining USN SH-3As, SH-3Ds and SH-3Gs are being brought up to this standard. The US Navy currently operates eleven squadrons in the carrier-based ASW role, each with six SH-3D/Hs.

The latest in a long line of Sikorsky aircraft to be built under licence by Westland, the British version is based on the US Navy's S-61 airframe but 'under the skin' is a very different machine, intended to operate independently of surface ships when hunting and attacking submarines. This requirement led Westland to install a complete tactical centre and a full range of sensors. All Westland Sea Kings are fitted with two Rolls-Royce Gnome turboshafts, based on the General Electric T58 used in the S-61.

The original Sea King HAS.1 ordered for the Royal Navy flew in 1969, and 56 were delivered by mid-1972. Twenty-one HAS.2s were then built, and all ▶

Left: Sikorsky SH-3D ASW helicopter of US Navy squadron HS-2. The starboard sponson houses the MAD 'bird' and the yellow disc is the drogue. 106 of this version were built in the USA and another 61 in Italy. The current version is the SH-3H.

Below: A Westland-built Sea King of the Royal Australian Navy. The Sea King was the first ASW helicopter with enough cabin space and lift to enable a full suite of sensors, weapons, displays and operators to be carried. It is thus capable of truly autonomous operations, unlike earlier ASW helicopters.

▶ HAS.1s modified to the new standard; all these are now being brought up to the latest HAS.5 standard. Search radar of the HAS.2 and HAS.5 is the AW.391, the dorsal radome of which gives the cabin its recognisable 'hump'; this will later be replaced by the MEL 'Sea Searcher', the antenna for which requires a larger radome. The Plessey Type 195 dunking sonar is supplemented by Ultra Electronics miniature sonobuoys. In the HAS.5 the resulting data will be handled by an advanced Marconi Avionics LAPADS acoustic processing and display system.

Armament includes up to four homing torpedoes—either US Mk 46 or the new Marconi Stingray 'smart' homing torpedo—or four Mk 11 depth

Above: Mk 42 Sea King as supplied to the Indian Navy. Westland have supplied Sea Kings to ten countries.

charges; it is also probable that nuclear depth bombs can be carried under certain circumstances. ASW versions of the Westland Sea King have been sold to India and Australia.

A squadron of nine HAS.2/5 Sea Kings operates from each of the Royal Navy's anti-submarine carriers, and HAS.2s are also deployed on the Royal Fleet Auxiliaries of the Fort Grange class.

Below: Westland Sea King HAS Mk 5 which has the Marconi LAPADS (lightweight acoustic processing and display system), improved radar, better avionics and many other changes.

153

Sikorsky SH-60B Seahawk
(USA)

Type: Shipborne ASW helicopter (crew of 3).
Dimensions: Fuselage length 50ft (15·2m); main rotor diameter 53·7ft (16·4m); height 17·2ft (5·2m).
Weight: Empty 13,648lb (6,191kg); maximum 21,884lb (9,926kg).
Engines: Two 1,690shp General Electric T700-401 turboshafts.
Performance: Maximum speed 126kt (234km/h); service ceiling 18,500ft (5,639m); mission endurance 3½hr.
Payload: 2 Mk 46 homing torpedoes.

The Sikorsky SH-60B Seahawk is the basis of the US Navy's LAMPS III ASW system for operation from cruisers, destroyers and frigates. The aircraft is a variant of the US Army's UH-60A, developed under the Utility Tactical Transport Aircraft System (UTTAS) project. The Navy aircraft has different landing gear from the Army model and folding systems for the main rotor and tail, both of which are required for operations from small ships at sea. The aircraft features an advanced rotor design and an engine built from individual modules which can be replaced by nine common tools. A RAST (Recovery, Assist, Secure and Traverse) haul-down and handling system is also under development, to enable the SH-60B to land in sea conditions up to Sea State 5. The first SH-60Bs out of a projected total of 204 were ordered in April 1982, and deliveries began in 1983.

Below: One of the development SH-60Bs with non-standard nose-probe on a flight test. Note sensor arrays beneath the nose.

Above: SH-60B parked on the flight-deck of the USS *Arthur W Radford*, a Spruance class destroyer. Note the sweep-back on the rotor tips.

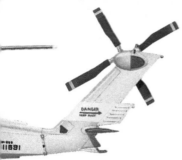

Left: This SH-60B profile shows the 5 by 5 pneumatic launcher for sonobuoys and the radome in the nose. The SH-60B is the air portion of the LAMPS III programme and is based on the UH-60A airframe, although the degree of commonality is small.

The primary LAMPS mission is ASW, and the aircraft carries an extensive avionics suite developed by an industrial team headed by IBM. The main sensors are a Texas Instruments APS-124 search radar in the forward section of the fuselage, an ASQ-81 towed MAD system, a UYS-1 acoustic processor and an ALQ-142 ESM system. Two Mk 46 lightweight torpedoes can be carried on pylons, and a 25-tube sonobuoy launcher is fitted on the port side of the fuselage.

The LAMPS III system is ship-based: overall control remains with the parent ship, which also processes data from the helicopter's own sensors. SH-60B operations are monitored by an acoustic sensor operator (ASO) in the ship's sonar room and a remote radar operator (REMRO) and an electronic warfare operator (EWO) in the ship's Combat Information Centre (CIC). There is also an air tactical control officer (ATACO) who co-ordinates the activities of the three operators and who is, in effect, the tactical mission commander. The SH-60B has a crew of three: pilot, airborne tactical officer (ATO)—who monitors the ship's tactical direction of the mission—and sensor operator.

Secondary LAMPS missions include anti-ship surveillance and targeting, vertical replenishment, medical evacuation and search and rescue. The US Navy plans to buy some 200 SH-60B helicopters for service aboard guided-missile frigates (e.g. Perry class), Aegis-equipped guided-missile destroyers and Spruance class ASW destroyers.

ASW Weapons Systems

Ikara (Australia)

Ikara is a system in which a guided missile is used to carry a torpedo to the vicinity of a submarine target, thus cutting down dramatically on the 'dead time' between the acquisition of the target and the arrival of the weapon. The missile is launched from a surface warship and flies at high subsonic speed out to a maximum range of some 12 miles (20km). A data link back to the ship ensures that the missile flies to the computer-predicted optimum launch point, where the torpedo is released, makes a parachute descent to the sea and then carries out a normal homing attack on the target. Mk 44 and Mk 46 torpedoes are among those which can be carried, and the system is in service with the Australian, Brazilian and Royal Navies.

Above: An Ikara being prepared for flight. The white missile acts as a carrier for the ASW torpedo slung underneath.

L5 Multipurpose Torpedo (France)

This torpedo is in service with the French and Belgian Navies. It is powered by silver-zinc batteries and has a speed of some 35kt, which suggests that its capability against modern, fast, Soviet submarines is marginal. It has an active/passive head capable of homing attacks, either direct or in programmed search.

Above: French Navy frigate *Detroyat*. The caps of the fixed tubes for L5 torpedoes can be seen on the after deckhouse.

Type A 184 Torpedo (Italy)

This wire-guided torpedo can be launched from surface ships or submarines against either surface or submarine targets. It has a range of some 8·7 miles (14km) and a speed of some 35kt. The torpedo is controlled from the launching ship until its own acoustic sensors acquire the target, when it is allowed to carry out a normal homing attack. The A 184 is in service with the Italian Navy.

Bofors Type 375 Rocket System

Developed in Sweden, this rocket system is in service with at least eight navies. The missile weighs some 551lb (250kg) and carries 220lb (100kg) of TNT or 176lb (80kg) of hexotonal. The launcher has either two or four tubes and is automatically reloaded from an operating room below; fuzes are set automatically at proximity, time or impact. The missile has a rocket motor and follows a flat trajectory, thus minimising time of flight. Maximum range is approximately 4,000yd (3,657m).

SS-N-14 (Silex) (USSR)

The SS-N-14 is fitted on most modern, large Soviet surface warships. The system appears similar in concept to the Ikara (qv) in that a missile carries a torpedo to the vicinity of a target where it is dropped to carry out a normal search and homing attack. The Soviet missile is 24·6ft (7·6m) long and is fired from either a twin-arm launcher (e.g. *Moskva*) or from a quadruple bin (e.g. *Udaloy*). The flight profile shows a height of about 2,500ft (750m) and a speed of Mach 0·95, for a maximum range of 34 miles (55km). SS-N-14 is believed to have an alternative nuclear warhead, whilst the homing torpedo version may also have an anti-ship capability.

SS-N-15/16 (USSR)

The SS-N-15 is thought to be fitted to Soviet attack submarines of the Alfa, Papa, Tango, Kilo and Victor-III classes, and may well be fitted to others as well. It is an ASW system similar to the US SUBROC in which an underwater-launched missile travels to the surface, follows an airborne flight path and then releases a depth bomb (SS-N-15) or a homing torpedo (SS-N-16). Maximum range is estimated to be about 34 miles (55km).

ASW Rocket Launchers (USSR)

Virtually all Soviet surface warships carry at least one ASW rocket launcher, of which there are several varieties. The rockets are fired in a predetermined pattern from a multiple launcher which is remotely trained and elevated. Current models include the RBU 1800 (a 5-barrelled 250mm system used in older ships); RBU 2500 (16-barrelled 250mm system, fitted in older cruisers and destroyers and in some small escorts); RBU 4500A (6-barrelled 300mm system with automatic loading); RBU 6000 (300mm system with barrels arranged in a circular fashion; range about 6,560yd [6,000m]; fitted in many modern warships); and RBU 1200 (6-barrelled system, fitted on the quarters of larger warships; may have an anti-torpedo role).

Above: Among the weapons on the foredeck of the Soviet battlecruiser *Kirov* are the twin-tube launchers for the SS-N-14 anti-submarine missile.

Above: A very clear view of an RBU 6000 ASW rocket launcher. There is a great variety of this type of launcher fitted on virtually every Soviet warship.

Stingray (UK)

Stingray can be launched from helicopters, fixed-wing aircraft and surface ships, and is now in service with the Royal Navy. It is an autonomous acoustic-homing torpedo and is claimed to be equally effective in shallow and deep water. An on-board computer can make its own tactical decisions during the course of an attack.

ASROC (USA)

ASROC consists of a nuclear depth bomb (approx 1KT) or a Mk 46 torpedo attached to a solid-propellant rocket motor. It is fired either from a box-shaped 8-cell launcher or from the Mk 10 Terrier launcher. On launch, the missile follows a ballistic trajectory and the rocket motor is jettisoned at a predetermined point. If the payload is a torpedo it descends by parachute to the surface, where its homing head and motor are activated; a depth bomb free-drops and is detonated at a set depth. Range is estimated to be 1·25–6·2 miles (2–10km). This very successful system is in service on some 240 ships of twelve navies. A vertically launched version is now under development.

Above: ASROC missile at the moment of launch from the foredeck of a US frigate. Payload is either a Mk 46 torpedo or a nuclear depth bomb.

Right: Having been launched underwater, SUBROC is now in the air portion of its mission, prior to the torpedo returning to the ocean.

SUBROC (USA)

SUBROC is a nuclear missile (1KT warhead) designed for use against hostile SSBNs. It is launched from a standard torpedo tube and after a short underwater journey it rises to the surface and becomes airborne until it returns to the water and the warhead sinks to a set depth before detonating. Range is about 35 miles (56km) and airborne speed in excess of Mach 1; estimated lethal radius of the W-55 warhead is 3–5 miles (5–8km). Some USN SSNs are equipped to carry SUBROC; each carries 4–6 missiles. SUBROC is scheduled to be replaced by ASW–SOW (qv) in the late 1980s.

ASW-SOW (USA)

The Anti-Submarine Warfare Stand-Off Weapon (ASW-SOW) is designed to replace the SUBROC system (qv); it may also be available for launch from surface ships. The missile will be stored in a canister in a standard torpedo tube and on launch the entire canister will leave the submarine and travel to the surface, where the missile motor will ignite, the canister will detach itself and the missile proceed towards the target. The payload will be the new Advanced Lightweight Torpedo (ALWT), a Mk 46 torpedo (surface ships) or a nuclear depth bomb.

Above: A Boeing ASW-SOW replica test capsule is loaded aboard a submarine for a test firing. This weapon is due to replace the SUBROC.

Above: One of the extremely successful Mk 46 torpedoes installed on an SH-3. This weapon is in use with at least 21 navies.

Mk 46 Torpedo (USA)

This torpedo is used by at least 21 navies, and is a deep-diving, high-speed device which can be launched from surface warships, helicopters or fixed-wing aircraft; it can also be carried by the ASROC and Ikara systems (qv). The Mk 46 has an active/passive acoustic homing sensor for its role of submarine attack. The increased speed of Soviet SSNs, allied to the new Clusterguard paint which seriously attenuates the acoustic response, has given rise to the Near-Term Improvement Program (NEARTIP) which will be both applied to new-production Mk 46s and retrofitted to in-service torpedoes. The Mk 46 is also used in the CAPTOR system, in which an encapsulated torpedo (hence 'CAPTOR') is moored in deep water and then launched on detection of a suitable hostile target. These mines can be delivered by surface ships, aircraft or submarines.

Above CAPTOR mines loaded on a P-3 Orion. Traditional mines wait for a target to approach within range, but the CAPTOR launches its Mk 46 torpedo actively to hunt its target.

Advanced Lightweight Torpedo (ALWT) (USA)

The latest Soviet submarines are not only faster and capable of diving deeper than previous types, but are also being constructed of new, stronger materials. In addition, they are being coated with anechoic paint or even (it has been suggested) anechoic tiles to reduce the reflective signature. Thus although in-service torpedoes can be improved to a certain extent, the challenge is now such that a totally new torpedo is needed; the current US programme is called ALWT. This is expected to have a similar size and weight to the Mk 46, although every effort is being made to increase the vital element of speed. A stored chemical energy propulsion system (SCEPS) is used, and it is intended to use a directed-energy warhead to achieve the required penetration of target hulls.

OTHER SUPER-VALUE MILITARY GUIDES IN THIS SERIES......

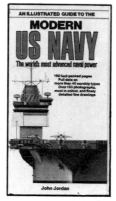

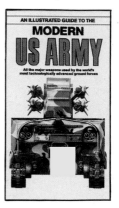

OTHER ILLUSTRATED MILITARY GUIDES NOW AVAILABLE.